ROBERT C. CROSBY is senior pastor of The Christian Center in Burlington, Massachusetts, where he lives with his wife and four children. He is the author of *Now We're Talking! Questions That Bring You Closer to Your Kids* and *Now We're Talking! Questions to Build Intimacy with Your Spouse.*

"The mass of men live lives of quiet desperation."

—*Henry David Thoreau*

Acknowledgments

No book is ever written by one man. A book is a collective synthesis of what a writer has seen, heard, experienced, been taught, and of what he, too, has read. I am deeply indebted to the host of "investors" who have a good deposit of insight in me. What a joy it is to fellowship with the great minds of great souls in the pages they have penned. Their writings have caused me to think, to ponder, and to observe.

Like no other writing project I have undertaken, this one has been difficult to complete. My notion is that any work which focuses on the soul is as such primarily because the soul is forever growing. My hope is that mine is expanding, as I feel today that the book is more complete than yesterday and am suspicious that it would be better a year from now.

It is the temptation to write the "final word" on a subject that keeps men from completing books . . . ever. Having heard that counsel, I have resisted that temptation and chosen a day to say, "It is unfinished . . . but ready." I trust that this leg of my journey will encourage you on to the next leg of yours. Thus, this is obviously not a "final" word . . . merely a word on the intriguing nature of a man's soul.

David Hazard has been more than an editor on this journey: he's been a "soul brother" in the truest sense. Also, I am grateful to Jack Caputo for giving the rough draft a hard read and pointing out some "outstanding" observations. And I don't know what I would have done without the steady encouragement and enthusiasm of my soul mate, Pamela.

Contents

Foreword

Soul is a word that is becoming important to us again. It has re-entered our culture, showing up on the covers of books and magazines, as the topic of talk-shows and conferences. These days, soul is not only in our hearts, it is fresh on our minds.

It seems we are awakening to the need for something more, or is it *Someone*? On the upside, it's encouraging to watch our preoccupations with outward signs of success (i.e., positions and possessions) being castigated for leaving us unfulfilled and empty. We are finding that the American dream cannot satisfy a soul. We find ourselves in pursuit of a deeper, more meaningful life. We ache for purpose and perspective.

On the downside, the empty void within men is doing more than merely evoking a truckload of heartfelt questions; it has issued a broad invitation to every would-be definer of soul, of spirit, and of life. Into this chasm is pouring a deluge of commentary and advice on how to live life more soulfully. Unfortunately, much of what is coming under the covers of "soul" by way of print and philosophy is in the form of a *stew* of what man has observed rather than a *lens* into what God has revealed. Several authors have carefully gleaned "soul principles" from every religion and persuasion and shaped them into broad-brushed compilations on the human spirit. Such volumes, I believe, have only whetted our internal hunger. They have created more questions than answers. I sincerely hope that this volume accomplishes something more.

Our souls crave more than the contemplations of man. They deeply desire the revelation of God. His Word. His touch. His company. May you come to know these more and more. May you experience Him more and more as you live life deep and true . . . from the soul.

PART ONE

A Living Soul
(The Man God *Chooses*)

CHAPTER ONE

Living Life From the Soul

"And the LORD God formed man of the dust of the ground, and breathed into his nostrils the breath of life; and man became a living soul."

Genesis 2:7, KJV

"The tragedy of man is not that we die, but that which dies in us while we still live."

—Albert Schweitzer

Men were designed to live life one way—from the soul.

By this I mean that we were designed to live for more than physiological fulfillment. Food, shelter, clothing, and sex turn out not to be enough. We hunger for other things—purpose, intimacy, acceptance, fulfillment, and some way to make a lasting contribution. Our soulless world deceives us into thinking we can fill these inner voids in other ways—by cultivating a charming or impressive appearance, by pumping money into our bank account, or by loading more possessions into a bigger house. We imagine that owning and achieving will satisfy the hungers of the inner man.

And yet, with each new "piece of the pie" we attain, we soon find ourselves wanting, feeling as if we are missing something. More often than not, we are left with confused thoughts and opinions about what we should do to satisfy our seemingly bottomless appetite for respect, meaning, acceptance, admiration, and approval. And deeper than all of that, to satisfy our starvation for a love that will not turn us away and abandon us on our own.

How do we live life from the soul—in a way that helps us fill the needs of our inner man? We seem to be trained in every other skill and pursuit imaginable. But rarely are we taught how to grow a living, healthy soul.

When the Bible speaks of the soul, it is referring to the inner life of a man, to that which is within. In the Genesis account, the effect of God's breathing into man was the creation of a "living soul" (2:7). David says, in a state of awe at God's intimate workings, "For you have created my inmost being"—referring to the pattern of passions and instincts and desires as unique to David as his fingerprints (see Psalm 139). It would seem that the soul of man is not only God-designed, but God-given and God-breathed.

And although we were graced by God with a "living soul," it is also true that the internal passions, instincts, and desires that comprise our soul can easily mislead us. By natural inclination, when apart from God we act in ways that go against Him and against other people. In short, our tendency as we take on life is to ignore God and misuse people all in an attempt to get one thing—our own way. By the time we reach adulthood, we have become stubbornly entrenched in a path of our own choosing—apart from the God who could direct us to our purpose and isolated from the people who could give us the intimacy and support we crave. Separated from a true relationship with God, our inner impulses are disordered, like crazy spark plugs misfiring, giving us and everyone around us a rough ride.

Living life from the soul is not an evil or misbegotten, self-centered pursuit. Not when God is brought back into our lives to do a reordering. But it does mean learning how to come face-to-face with who we truly are in the depths of our being, seeing ourselves under the light of God's wisdom. And it means learning how to reconnect and complete our manhood by allowing the character of Christ to grow in us—to bring the tempering, balancing, stabilizing influence of grace and godliness to subdue and redirect our impulses and motivations. By embracing the life that Christ offers—that is, the attitude of self-surrender (soul surrender) to God—what is disordered, confused, self-serving, and immature about us can become directed, clear, self-giving, and mature.

As Christians, we sometimes mistakenly think that the moment a man commits his life to God in Christ he is changed instantly into a perfect specimen of manhood. Some men do experience dramatic changes, but they are not always deep or lasting. And many men are left to secretly wonder why—in their deepest heart of hearts, where anger and fantasies and exaggerated visions of winning at another's expense fester—there seems to be little change at all.

Many men miss the first important step: We don't know how to come face-to-face with who we are in the depths of our being. We are masters of avoiding the truth about ourselves. We refuse to look squarely at the man within who is indeed incomplete and wanting and misguided apart from God.

But when we do—when we stand before God, vulnerable as children once again—we experience a strong embrace and a bold, deep, all-encompassing love that changes us. A love that makes us the grown men we want to be.

When we learn to live with God, to walk closely with Him, we find within us a *presence* that fills our emptiness. And we discover that there are resources we can tap to find a virtually inexhaustible supply of strength, motivation, wisdom, and character from which to create a rich life, one pleasing to God.

I have watched men come alive to it. When men finally find soul potential—that inward capacity for spiritual insight and power—they are amazed at the reservoir of new life they find within. It is a wonder to behold and a blessing to experience when a man truly reconnects from the soul to the heart of God.

The Man Within

When I speak of man's *soul* I am referring to his inward life or self. The inner life is marked by our vital drives and desires. It is the seat of our mind, our will, our passions, and our emotions—a *thermostat* of sorts. Our soul can be corrupted by the influence of the world and sin, or it can be powerfully shaped by the influence of God's Spirit and His Word.

The soul of man is the part of him that is awakened, enlivened, and transformed through a personal relationship with God through Jesus Christ. When a man takes on a Christ-centered lifestyle and commitment, he discovers that his soul breaks open into a fire storm of purpose, power, and godly passion. As new life pours from within, it can fill his entire life and richly bless those around him. One of the central messages of the Bible is that God wants every man, through His Son's example, to rediscover what it means to come out of hiding into His real presence and to live life from the soul.

Most of us experience the soul as a kind of *thermometer*—registering cool, warm, or hot emotions. That thermometer tells us how we're feeling inside, but it can seem as if it's controlled by everyone else but us as people and circumstances change our inner setting to PEACE or

ANXIETY, LOVE or ANGER, JOY or FRUSTRATION, FAITH or FEAR.

But other people do not really control us. Neither do circumstances—not in the ultimate sense. There are a host of influences and forces that can press in, but we can monitor and regulate what comes out of our heart. John Wesley exemplified such discipline when he wrote: "I have determined to do nothing without calmness of spirit."

More often we allow our souls to function like thermometers; that is, we say, "I can't *help* how I feel. That made me mad, and I just lost it. If you don't like it, too bad." But as we allow God into our innermost being, He shows us the truth about our reactions to life. In His light we gain understanding about what irks us, saddens us, or fills us with soul-splitting happiness. He puts us in control of the *thermostat* of our soul and restores our sense of inner regulation.

Consider the word picture created here—the difference between a thermometer and a thermostat. A thermometer *fluctuates* as frequently as its surrounding conditions change. It is at the mercy of outer conditions. At times it freezes, at others it boils. But a thermostat *regulates* temperature; it is not governed by it. Regardless of the surrounding conditions, a well-oiled thermostat maintains a consistent "cool" when things heat up and a certain "warmth" when things grow cold. The soul of a man who walks in God's Spirit is a thermostat. It can sustain him through the worst crises. Outside of God's Spirit, a man's soul can let loose the fire of hell itself.

Let's look now at some of the unregulated impulses by which a man's life can be motivated. Consider these carefully:

- When a man lives out of his anger, he *alienates* the people in his life.
- When a man lives out of his self-centered ambition, he *neglects* the people in his life.
- When a man lives out of his wounds, he *hurts* the people in his life.
- When a man lives out of his fears, he *overlooks* the people in his life.
- When a man lives out of his discouragement, he *rejects* the people in his life.
- When a man lives out of his greed, he *undervalues* the people in his life.
- When a man lives out of his lusts, he *uses* the people in his life.
- When a man lives out of his prejudices, he *offends* the people in his life.

On the other hand, when a man lives out of his soul—the character of Christ directing his impulses—he *blesses* the people in his life.

Soft Males—Hard Men

In *Iron John*, Robert Bly's modern classic on the struggles of manhood, he refers to the type of males that emerged in the 1970s:

> I began to see all over the country a phenomenon that we might call the "soft male." Sometimes, even today, when I look out at an audience, perhaps half the young males are what I'd call soft. They're lovely, valuable people—I like them—they're not interested in harming the earth or starting wars. There's a gentle attitude toward life in their whole being and style of living.
>
> But many of these men are not happy. You quickly notice the lack of energy in them. They are life-preserving but not exactly life-giving. Ironically, you often see these men with strong women who positively radiate energy.[1]

There is a difference between being soft and being sensitive. Softness is an apologetic approach to life, which springs from a man's own insecurities or weaknesses. It is not action but *reaction*. Sensitivity, on the other hand, flows out of a certain strength from the soul of a man who has a sense of purpose, a man at peace with God and with himself. It comes through as the solid influence of a tender spirit with firm commitments.

Newsweek carried a report on what it called "the new wave of mountain men." Presently, there are some 60,000 serious mountain climbers in the United States. Within this group, however, is an elite upper echelon of climbers known as "hard men." For them the rigor of climbing mountains and scaling sheer rock faces is a way of life. As a matter of fact, to many of them climbing is a part of their overall commitment to life. They would tell you that inching their way up granite, alone and with death at their backs, has taught them much about life. To this rare breed, the ultimate experience is called free-soloing: climbing with no equipment and no safety ropes.

John Baker is considered by his peers to be the best of the hard men. He has free-soloed some of America's most difficult rock faces with no safety or climbing equipment whatsoever. John Baker would be the first to tell you that his skill has not come easily. It has been acquired and developed through commitment, dedication, and training. It flows from more than his technique alone; it is housed within the confines of his soul. John's whole life and accomplishments are regulated by a focused desire, a passion.

Recently, Billy Graham asked the question, "Where are the hard men

. . . for Jesus? Where are those who will bring all their energies to bear for the sake of Christ? That's the kind of people it's going to take to spread the gospel around the world. . . ."

In the eighteenth century, John Wesley said, "Give me one hundred preachers who fear nothing but sin and desire nothing but God, and I care not a straw whether they be clergymen or laymen; such alone will shake the gates of hell and set up the kingdom of heaven on earth."

Solomon asked a piercing question that still echoes today: "Many a man claims to have unfailing love, but a faithful man who can find?" (Proverbs 20:6).

If we want to live life from the soul—focused by the power of His life and energy, not flabby and dissipated by our own disordered impulses—we must begin by surrendering our own purposes to reconnect with God's purposes. Walking with Him means discovering the reason we were made, letting His light shine on the walls within our soul so we can read the destiny He inscribed there with His own finger.

Do you want to be this kind of man? Controlled by a destiny, sensitive to God and others, firm in purpose and mission?

You can be. But it depends on choice. Your choice.

You see, the choice to let God into your innermost man and empower you—or to keep Him out—is in *your* hands.

A Tale of Two Men

Stephen, the church's first martyr, would definitely qualify as one of Billy Graham's "hard men for Jesus." He was a man who lived life with a strong soul-attachment to God, a man who lived life from an inner, God-empowered reservoir of strength. He was not a pastor—he was an ordinary man who possessed an extraordinary spirit. And so the apostles made him their first choice to serve as a deacon. As he comforted the needy of the church, he showed his true character—a man full of compassion, who was faithful, diligent, godly, and trustworthy. A man strong and whole enough to escape his own petty ego-needs to help and strengthen other people. The Bible introduces us to Stephen in this way:

> They chose Stephen, a man full of faith and of the Holy
> Spirit. . . . Now Stephen, a man full of God's grace and power,
> did great wonders and miraculous signs among the people . . .
> but [men] could not stand up against his wisdom or the Spirit
> by whom he spoke (Acts 6:5, 8, 10).

Then someone in the community conspired against Stephen and

falsely accused him of blasphemy. Seized and arrested, he faced his murderous accusers. Consider the full picture of Stephen in the moment when his life hung in the balance:

All who were sitting in the Sanhedrin [the ruling Jewish elders of the day] looked intently at Stephen, and they saw that his face was like the face of an angel (Acts 6:15).

How do you picture a godly man—a man with "the face of an angel"? Indeed there must have been some radiant power beaming from the intensity of his eyes. But consider the boldness and challenge of his words. Standing before the best-trained Jewish scholars of his day, Stephen broke into a confrontive and articulate discourse, taking these spiritually myopic men from the Old Testament to the New, from Moses to the Messiah, painting a vivid picture of Jesus as the true Christ (Acts 7:2–50). Then this man with the face of an angel looked them squarely in the eyes and said:

You stiff-necked people, with uncircumcised hearts and ears! You are just like your fathers: You always resist the Holy Spirit! Was there ever a prophet your fathers did not persecute? They even killed those who predicted the coming of the Righteous One. And now you have betrayed and murdered [Jesus] . . ." (Acts 7:51–52).

With his life in the balance, Stephen went for broke. Most of us would have gone for self-preservation. But Stephen was a *free-solo* kind of man. Why? Because the most basic impulses of his soul—even the will to live and not die—were controlled by the hand of God. Stephen had chosen to surrender all.

Immediately, upon considering this story, I want to step back in time and ask Stephen a hundred questions: Weren't you afraid? If so, how did you overcome that fear? What disciplines/experiences in your life kept you so "full of the Holy Spirit and faith"? What did it take for you to resist your natural impulses as a man in this situation and respond to God's prompting? How did you keep from simply fighting fire with fire? Were you ever tempted to back down? How did you manage to control your temper? When facing the greatest conflict of your life, how were you able to "see" Christ so clearly in the midst of such difficulty (cf. 7:55–56)?

No doubt, Stephen knew his challenge would be explosive. He was right:

When [the religious leaders] heard this, they were furious

and gnashed their teeth at him. But Stephen, full of the Holy Spirit, looked up to heaven and saw the glory of God, and Jesus standing at the right hand of God. "Look," he said, "I see heaven open and the Son of Man standing at the right hand of God."

At this they covered their ears and, yelling at the top of their voices, they all rushed at him, dragged him out of the city and began to stone him (Acts 7:54–58).

Stephen never stood taller than on the day he fell. As his body was pelted to death with stones, his soul was ushered into heaven by Christ himself. So aware was he of Christ—so full of life, so sure of his purpose, priority, and passion—that he could draw upon these inner resources in the very hour of death. Stephen stands before every man as proof that we can rise above our impulses and live life from the strength of a surrendered soul.

In contrast to Stephen—just a few feet away, but in spirit a world apart—stood Saul. Saul was as passionate about stamping out Christians as Stephen was passionate to let the light of Christ burn in him. Saul was just the kind of angry young man the Sanhedrin needed to do its dirty work. We meet him in this manner:

> Meanwhile [as Stephen was being stoned by Saul's cohorts], the witnesses laid their clothes at the feet of a young man named Saul . . . [who was] giving approval to his death. . . .
> Godly men buried Stephen and mourned deeply for him. But Saul began to destroy the church. Going from house to house, he dragged off men and women and put them in prison (Acts 7:58–60; 8:2–3).

Saul—a zealot's kind of "man's man"—made a name for himself by crusading all over Palestine, torturing Christians in an effort to prove how right and how powerful he was.

And then, in the time it takes for lightning to strike, Saul was changed. The God he claimed to represent showed up and took a walk, as it were, through Saul's soul. Take a walk through that soul with me, following the steps of God, to see what it took for Saul's heart to be reharnessed to its true and greatest purpose.

How a Man Finds His Path in Christ

Many of the motivations that drove Saul, as he set out on his self-chosen, self-directed mission to vanquish an "enemy" and win a name for himself, are the same motivations that show up in many men's lives today. The story of God's light-out-of-heaven confrontation with Saul on the road to Damascus is recorded in Acts 9. Can you see anything of yourself in this account?

First, Saul was mounted on his own "high horse." He was self-confident as he set off on his mission. Single-minded and self-assured, he was blinded by his own sense that he was right. Approaching Damascus, he was apparently riding high on his successes, his ambitions, his drivenness, and his accomplishments. He was a man whose will and drive and energy were harnessed to *pride.*

Second, his self-will allowed little room for compassion. Thinking he had the situation all sized up, Saul was determined to advance his own cause by destroying everyone else's. It appears that he was more bent on proving himself right than on actually discovering *the truth.* We see a man living out of his own *ambition.*

Third, he was trying to crush the very power that wanted to save him—the power of Love. Saul endeavored to overcome a movement powered by Love itself, with rage, force, and control. Living out of his free-ranging *anger,* Saul was determined to crush and subdue these opponents.

Fourth, he was stuck in gear and beyond reason. Living out of his own *stubbornness,* Saul was not willing to deal with his dilemma in the open-minded arena of debate and discussion. He had no patience for that. There was no listening, no compromising, and no cooperating—simply a seek-out-and-destroy mentality.

Finally, he was determined to punish anyone who disagreed with him. Living out of his *intolerance,* Saul's reasoning led him to this conclusion: "If they won't think my way, I'll exercise my power and make them pay."

Saul had a win/lose mentality. Surrender was not in his vocabulary. What was worse: he thought—no, he was *sure*—he was God's man doing the best he knew to do . . . all for God.

Sometimes the most difficult person to reach is the very religious person. You don't have to look very far in the Gospels to discover that Jesus' greatest source of frustration was not the "lost," the "heathen," the "sick," the "pagan," or the "poor": it was the most religious men of his day. They had all the right Scriptures between their ears, and they could rattle off correct doctrine. But without that deep soul surrender to God, it did them no good. Jesus saw right through them.

That's the way it is for many spiritual men today. You don't have to be abusive like Saul to slip into self-confident self-righteousness. You

merely have to forget that "the steps of a righteous man are ordered by
the Lord" (Psalm 37:23). You simply have to put your life on autopilot,
forget that real growth comes out of a changing spirit, and put on the
appearance of dedication. *You only have to forget that the real Christian
life is lived from the soul.*

When writers seek to describe a life-changing event in a person's life,
they will often refer to it as a "Damascus-road experience." On his way
to that city, Saul was knocked off his "high horse" when a sudden light
from heaven flashed around him. Then he heard the voice of Jesus, challenging and correcting him. Powerless and struck blind, Saul had to be
led by the hand the rest of the way, probably on foot. He had set out
powerful and self-assured; he entered Damascus helpless as a child,
waiting for Jesus to tell him what to do next. Jesus had instructed him:
"Now get up and go into the city, and you will be told what you must
do" (Acts 9:6).

In Damascus, Saul underwent a radical change. He was even ren-
amed *Paul*. But what did *not* change was Paul's essential nature. He still
had passion, drive, and zeal—some might even say *stubbornness*. But
now these attributes were tamed by God's hand. Redirected to the purpose of building rather than hurting. As God used Stephen's passion for
the needy, now he would use Paul's passion for theological truth.

God turned on the light in Stephen's soul in a moment of pain and
testing. God shone the light into Saul's soul in a moment of stubborn
pride. Both are examples of what God can do in a man's life when we
open all that's in us to Him. When we're willing to give our strength and
our breath, our dreams and our drive, for His good purposes.

Two men. Poles apart. One, Stephen, facing harsh opposition and yet
emanating the same grace which only Christ, to that point, had so vividly and publicly modeled. The other, Saul, dishing out the obscenities
of his own soul in the form of brutal and unjust violence heaped upon
the body of a man of whom the world was not worthy. Seldom had men
observed a soul so full of hatred and unmitigated malice. One had
learned to live from the soul. The other, clearly, had not.

How about you? Are you living your life in a way that's deeply connected to God *from the soul*? That is, are your purposes, motives, and
relationships connected to His will? Are your habits consistent with,
and in support of, that first commitment we make as Christian men—to
live so as to reveal God to the world by our love and actions?

Throughout this book, we are going to explore ways we can open
ourselves more honestly, more bravely to God. From other men who
have walked this way before us, we know that the rewards—if we begin

to grow from within—are great. A tighter walk with God. A greater love for our wife and children. A more profound sense of purpose. New "brothers" in spirit—men who are committed to us, no matter what. Isn't that the kind of life you want?

SOUL OPENER

Drawing Closer to God

"My soul is in anguish. How long, O Lord, how long?"

Psalm 6:3

"Unless in the first waking moment of the day you learn to fling the door wide back and let God in, you will work on a wrong level all day; but swing the door wide open and pray to your Father in secret, and every public thing will be stamped with the presence of God."[2]

—Oswald Chambers

Take some time to spend in prayer right now. Ask God to show you the "truth" about yourself. Be willing to accept the honest insights God wants to bring to you today. As a man, acknowledge that you have *something to face* in order to grow closer to God.

What sins are you wrestling with? Who is being hurt by them?

Take a look at the list below and be honest with yourself about the inner forces that drive the way you live and the way you approach relationships:

Most often I live
- ☐ out of my *anger*
- ☐ out of my *ambition*
- ☐ out of my *hurt*
- ☐ out of my *fear*
- ☐ out of my *discouragement*
- ☐ out of my *failures*
- ☐ out of my *greed*
- ☐ out of my *prejudice*
- ☐ out of my *lusts*
- ☐ out of my *bitterness*
- ☐ out of my _____.

Acknowledge the tendencies and drives within you. Confess them to God and seek His strength to overcome or direct them. Determine every day to set aside time to seek God in prayer and to commit your day to Him.

One great way to watch God at work in your life is to *keep a spiritual journal.* It doesn't have to be long or fancy. Keep it simple. As often as you can, jot down the date and some of the things you sense God confronting in you, and encouraging in you.

Months and years from now, you will be amazed at God's handiwork as He recreates and redirects you from the inside out.

Notes

1. As quoted in *Tender Warrior* by Stu Weber (Sisters, OR: Multnomah Books, 1993) pp. 70–71.
2. Oswald Chambers, *My Utmost for His Highest* (Westwood, CA: Barbour and Co., Inc., 1963), August 23, p. 173.

CHAPTER TWO

Soul at War

"Dear friends, I urge you, as aliens and strangers in the world, to abstain from sinful desires, which war against your soul."

1 Peter 2:11

"The essence of sin is to will one thing, for to set our will against the will of God is to dethrone God and make ourselves supreme in the little kingdom of Mansoul."[1]

—A. W. Tozer

"We are not human beings having a spiritual experience, but spiritual beings having a human experience."[2]

—Teilhard de Chardin

The apostle Paul was definitely "into" depth. His letters are filled with phrases like "in Christ," "through Christ," "fix your hearts . . . on things above," and so on.

There was nothing shallow about this man who had gone through a radical transformation. He had clearly journeyed to a deeper end of life's "pool" than most of us ever find. Because he had reconnected with God deeply, Paul was passionate about new life and grace. Consider a few of his rich expressions as he called Christians to stop splashing around in the shallows and come deeper into Christ:

> Oh, the depth of the riches of the wisdom and knowledge of God! How unsearchable his judgments, and his paths beyond tracing out! . . . For from him and through him and to him are all things. To him be the glory forever! Amen (Romans 11:33, 36).
>
> No eye has seen, no ear has heard, no mind has conceived what God has prepared for those who love him . . . but God

has revealed it to us by his Spirit (1 Corinthians 2:9–10).

I pray that you, being rooted and established in love, may have power, together with all the saints, to grasp how wide and long and high and deep is the love of Christ, and to know this love that surpasses knowledge—that you may be filled to the measure of all the fullness of God (Ephesians 3:17–19).

Why Do We Resist?

There is no doubt that Paul had regularly tasted in his life what Christ described when He said, "I have come that they may have life, and have it to the full" (John 10:10). And yet, amid all the marvelous heights of joy and spiritual insight, Paul was well acquainted with the resistance to God that still existed in himself. He knew what it was like to struggle with sin and to be pulled by tendencies to disobey God and His life principles. Eugene Peterson's translation of the New Testament, *The Message*, paints a picture of Paul's struggle that men can identify with. Listen in as his interior war rages:

> Yes, I'm full of myself—after all, I've spent a long time in sin's prison. What I don't understand about myself is that I decide one way, but then I act another, doing things I absolutely despise. So if I can't be trusted to figure out what is best for myself and then do it, it becomes obvious that God's command is necessary.
>
> *But I need something more!* For if I know the law but still can't keep it, and if the power of sin within me keeps sabotaging my best intentions, I obviously need help! I realize that I don't have what it takes. I can will it, but I can't *do* it. I decide to do good, but I don't *really* do it; I decide not to do bad, but then I do it anyway. My decisions, such as they are, don't result in actions. *Something has gone wrong deep within me and gets the better of me every time.*
>
> It happens so regularly that it's predictable. The moment I decide to do good, sin is there to trip me up. I truly delight in God's commands, but it's pretty obvious that not all of me joins in that delight. Parts of me covertly rebel, and just when I least expect it, they take charge.
>
> I've tried everything and nothing helps. I'm at the end of my rope. Is there no one who can do anything for me? Isn't that the real question? (Romans 7:14–24, emphasis mine).

Paul tells the truth about something I need to face in myself if I want to begin to reconnect with God from the soul. A part of me is hungry for more of God and the ability to do His will. Another part of me is so often intrigued with things that are opposed to His will. And so I find myself in a crossfire between a soul eager to emerge and a host of selfish desires determined to control. Between a beckoning Father and a relentless enemy.

Paul's cry is my cry: "I've tried everything and nothing helps. I'm at the end of my rope. Is there no one who can do anything for me?"

Soul Facts

As we try to answer Paul's question for ourselves, we have to step back from the immediate battlefield and understand the war we are in. Before trying to answer the question "How can I overcome the battle in my soul?" we can begin to find help as we answer more basic questions such as: *Why do I have a soul? Where did it come from? What is its purpose and potential? What is it for?* and *What does it take to harness and direct its energy and usefulness?*

The Bible gives us foundational truths about man's soul. It clearly points us to the beginning place of inner freedom and power.

Soul Fact #1—Man's soul emanates from God.

In a beautiful passage about the Savior that God would one day send, the Lord speaks: "Behold my servant, whom I uphold, my chosen, in whom my soul delights . . ." (Isaiah 42:1, RSV).

This invisible—but powerful—personhood of God is what we need to encounter. For it's the life of God that we need to sustain our soul. In truth, God at creation desired to place within man not only a soul, but a soul in the image of His own not only *a* spirit, but *His* Spirit.

Augustine, who spent his life observing the nature and function of the soul, wrote: "Just as we must acknowledge that the human soul is not what God is, so it must be set down that nothing is nearer to God among all the things he has created than the human soul."

Soul Fact #2—God places a soul into man, and every person possesses a soul.

Consider the account of God forming man from the elements of the earth and the breath of life from His soul: "The Lord God formed man from the dust of the ground, and breathed into his nostrils the breath of life; and man became a living soul" (Genesis 2:7, KJV). The Bible teaches us that "God is spirit" (John 4:24). The image of God within man is represented by the gift of *soul*—sometimes called *spirit*—which God placed within man. In essence, by this gift, God placed within every man a place set apart for His habitation, a place for Him to dwell. This is the purpose for your soul and mine.

Soul Fact #3—Men tend to lose their most valuable possession—their souls.

Though the soul was meant to house God in us, a tragic event took place—Adam and Eve's sin—which the Bible calls "the Fall." We all endorse their sin. We don't inherently want God's will and purpose for our lives. We want our own way. As a result, we push God *out* of the central core of our being, and we go out into the world to find other sources of fulfillment, respect, acceptance, and purpose. We look to our accomplishments, possessions, and to people in our lives to fill and fulfill us. And when they fail us, we are mystified.

In his orientation and relation toward the world, man becomes lost. Perhaps this is best illustrated by the grandmother who took her five-year-old grandson to Disney World. By early afternoon she had somehow lost him in a crowd. For hours and hours she searched frantically for him. She asked others to help her search, and they did. She sent out announcements over the loudspeakers in search of him, all to no avail. Finally, by the end of the day, she sat down exhausted on a bench and heard the sound of the marching band leading the parade down Main Street USA. She couldn't believe her eyes. There he was—her grandson—marching proudly to the beat of the music at the back of the band. Lost . . . and not even knowing it.

The most desolate of men is the one who has no sense of his own need for God. His life has so fit into the tunes and melodies of this world that he has forgotten God. He has "gained the world" and "lost his soul."

Jesus described this tragic confusion of man's nature and dilemma in the Gospel accounts in the form of a question: "What good will it be for a man if he gains the whole world, yet forfeits his soul? Or what can a man give in exchange for his soul?" (Matt. 16:26). The irony of man is that while desperately striving for the stuff the world offers, he notoriously tends to lose his own sense of identity, of purpose, of God in his life—his soul.

Soul Fact #4—Obedience to God begins at the level of the soul.

On at least one occasion Jesus was asked, "What is the most important commandment?" He swiftly responded, "Love the Lord your God with all your heart and with all your soul and with all your mind" (Matthew 22:37). Christ came not only to save the souls of men for eternity but to completely enliven and engage us in His purposes and presence in the here and now. He wants to enflame our souls with His passion and strength. These words of Christ make it clear that loving God involves much more than weekly attendance at a worship gathering. It requires the sum total of a man's heart, mind, and soul.

Soul Fact #5—Sin troubles and chokes the soul of man.

Sin is not just an alternative to what is good and right; sin strangles the inner man—strangles him to spiritual death if it can.

Sin diabolically subverts the purpose God has for a man's life. It short-circuits his strength and joy. Where God wants to build life-giving bonds, sin builds barriers—barriers between a man and God, between a man and his wife, his children, his peers.

Paul paints a stark contrast between the man who lives from a soul connected to God and the man who does not, and he does so in the light of God's judgment: "[At the judgment] to those who by persistence in doing good seek glory, honor and immortality, he will give eternal life. But for those who are *self-seeking* and who reject the truth and follow evil, there will be wrath and anger. There will be trouble and distress ... upon every soul of man that ... does evil ... but glory, honor and peace for everyone who does good ... (Romans 2:7–11 NIV, KJV, emphasis mine).

Soul Fact #6—Men must learn how to master sin.

You may recall that the first murder recorded in the Bible is when Cain killed his brother. God was pleased with the animal sacrifice Abel presented to him, but He rejected Cain's grain offering. Rather than surrender to God the right offering, Cain turned inward and fed on resentment, anger, and jealousy. Soon these impulses mastered him, and he brutally murdered his brother Abel. But not before he received a warning from God:

> Then the Lord said to Cain, "Why are you angry? Why is your face downcast? If you do what is right, will you not be accepted? But if you do not do what is right, sin is crouching at your door; it desires to have you, but you must master it" (Genesis 4:6–7).

God tried to coach Cain by urging him to connect his heart with God's own—by a willingness to obey in childlike innocence. Instead,

Cain pulled away from God to brood in his own anger, until it mastered him. And so the first murder took place on the earth.

Soul Fact #7—Men's souls are at war.

Peter straightforwardly addressed Christian men throughout the world when he penned this warning:

> Dear friends, I urge you, as aliens and strangers in the world, to abstain from sinful desires, which war against your soul (1 Peter 2:11).

Like Paul, Peter identifies man's struggle with sin as an internal war.

Interestingly enough, the remedy he suggests to overcoming sinful tendencies is *abstinence*. Do you see a situation that will make you angry, or enflame your lust? Don't go there! Or if it catches you unaware—leave the place at once. Don't dwell even in fantasies of lust or angry vengeance. He's saying, "Resist and avoid the tendencies to live out of your baser passions, and choose instead to live with your soul connected to God." Easier said than done, right?

Martin Luther offered his own advice regarding sinful thoughts: "You can't stop a bird from flying over your head, but you *can* stop it from building a nest in your hair."

Maybe we have not been trained in the simple steps that our loving Father has given us to help us walk away from the sin that would strangle and kill us.

The Solution

Soul Fact #8—If you are a Christian, freedom from sin comes from the inside out.

Paul not only painted a vivid picture of his battle with sin for us in Romans 7, he described a hopeful conclusion. He never denied the presence of *sin-potential* within himself—that would be naive and foolish, even deadly. But he learned that we can choose *not* to be overwhelmed by sin's threat.

Eugene Peterson translated Paul's solution to sin in wonderfully clear terms:

> The answer [to my battle with sin], thank God, is that Jesus Christ can and does [set us free from the law of sin and death]. . . . With the arrival of Jesus, the Messiah, that fateful

dilemma is resolved. Those who entered into Christ's being-here-for-us no longer have to live under a continuous, low-lying black cloud. A new power is in operation. The Spirit of life in Christ, like a strong wind, has magnificently cleared the air, freeing you from a fated lifetime of brutal tyranny at the hands of sin and death.

God went for the jugular when he sent his own Son. He didn't deal with the problem as something remote and un-important. In his Son, Jesus, He personally took on the human condition, entered the disordered mess of struggling humanity in order to set it right once and for all (Romans 7:25–8:3, *The Message*).

When Jesus enters into the life of a man, He proceeds to turn things upside-down—or should I say, "right side up." He says to every man, "It's okay to be honest with me about your drives, ambitions, lusts, and pride. I was a human being, too. I already *know* what you're feeling inside. Simply be honest with me *first*. Then I can show you why you don't need your anger, greed, or lustfulness to get you what you want. If you obey those impulses, you'll hurt other people and wound your own soul."

Because Jesus became a flesh-and-blood man, He calls us to himself. Then, as brother to brother, He confronts and challenges. He tears down and destroys. He builds and frees. When a man comes face-to-face with the grace and power of God, he is overwhelmed and undone. Christ leaves no stone unturned. With measured intensity He shakes all that can be shaken, so that which is unshakable—that is, eternal and strong—will remain (Hebrews 12:27).

You see, God is intent on our freedom and determined to light a flame of spiritual passion in every willing man. The Bible says "our God is a consuming fire" (Hebrews 12:29). When God spoke to a discouraged Moses and called him to leadership He "appeared to him in flames of fire" (Exodus 3:2). When He led a nation through the wilderness at night toward a land of promise, He did so as "a pillar of fire" (Exodus 14:24). When He brought Elijah into heaven He escorted him in a "chariot of fire" (2 Kings 2:11). It was John the Baptist who promised that Jesus would baptize men with "the Holy Spirit and with fire" (Matthew 3:11). And on the Day of Pentecost the followers of Christ were catapulted to action amid "tongues of fire" (Acts 2:3).

Being alive with the passion of God—cleansing our desires within, driving us to act in godliness—is what distinguishes a righteous man from the others. In such a soul, a fire is lit. The Holy Spirit causes a man to burn within for a deeper knowledge of Christ. An evidence that God has come close is to have a burning desire to tell others how to have a deep, heart-to-heart friendship with God.

The psalmist wrote, "He makes . . . flames of fire his servants" (Psalm 104:4). Jeremiah was so passionate about the Word of God that he described it as a "fire shut up in my bones" (Jeremiah 20:9). Jesus called a church to impassioned commitment when He said, "I know your deeds, that you are neither cold nor hot. I wish you were either one or the other! So, because you are lukewarm—neither hot nor cold—I am about to spit you out of my mouth" (Revelation 3:15–16).

A righteous man is one who is learning to love God with all of his "heart, soul, mind, and strength" (see Mark 12:30). As his devotion to God grows, a man's soul gains a greater capacity for faith, hope, and love. The Spirit of God not only opens a man's soul, He empowers it with the ability to believe (faith), the ability to endure (hope), and the ability to commune (love).

Isn't this what you want—rather than to be consumed by soul-fires out of control—to be fired with passion that gives you more life?

Soul Opener

Drawing Closer to God

"Have mercy on me, O God, have mercy on me, for in you my soul takes refuge. I will take refuge in the shadow of your wings until the disaster has passed."

Psalm 57:1

"Faith is the grit and soul that puts the dare into dreams."

—Max Lucado

Prayerfully consider and ask yourself the following questions:

1. In the battle for your soul, which side is winning? How can you tell?
2. What parts of you "covertly rebel" against God to this day?
3. As a man, what are the biggest struggles you contend with in life?
4. Are you gaining the world and losing your soul—or losing the world and gaining your soul? In what ways?

Men who choose to follow Christ soon learn that they have *something to resist*—namely, an enemy and a personal tendency toward sinful actions and reactions. According to the Bible, the most effective way to resist sin and Satan is to fill your heart and mind with the Word of God. Take some time now to pray over the areas of temptation and sin that you are prone to fall into, and speak these promises of God to your own soul:

> I can do all things through Christ who strengthens me (Philippians. 4:13, NKJV).

> So do not fear, for I am with you; do not be dismayed, for I am your God. I will strengthen you and help you; I will uphold you with my righteous right hand (Isa. 41:10).

> For though we live in the world, we do not wage war as the world does. The weapons we fight with are not the weapons of the world. On the contrary, they have divine power to demolish strongholds (2 Corinthians 10:3–4).

Pastor E. V. Hill cites Jesus' battle in the wilderness (Matt. 4) as he calls men to use the Word of God as a weapon to resist Satan:

> One of the most important things for us to learn is how to have the right conversation with the devil. . . . Respond the same way Jesus did: "It is written." Hit him with the Word. Hit him! Hit him! Hit him![3]

Open your weaknesses to God in prayer. Link up with Him by planting more and more of His life-giving, heart-freeing Word in your soul.

Notes

1. A. W. Tozer, *The Knowledge of the Holy* (Camp Hill, PA: Christian Publications, 1964), p. 37.
2. As quoted by Gordon MacDonald, *The Life God Blesses* (Nashville, TN: Thomas Nelson Publishers, 1994), p. 76.
3. From a message delivered at Promise Keepers rally in Boulder, CO.

CHAPTER THREE

Snapshots of the Soul Set Free

"If the Son sets you free, you will be free indeed."

John 8:36

"Once we roared like lions for liberty; now we bleat like sheep for security! The solution of America's problem is not in terms of big government, but it is in big men over whom nobody stands in control but God."

—Norman Vincent Peale

"Superficiality is the curse of our age. . . . The desperate need today is not for a greater number of intelligent people, or gifted people, but for deep people."[1]

—Richard Foster

When a man enters into a faith relationship with Jesus Christ, God begins to open his soul. A new power is "in operation" (Rom. 7:25). Instead of merely living out of his baser nature and instincts—greed, selfish ambition, competition, envy, lust—he has the chance to begin living out of motives much higher, more noble. He has a chance to experience life with spiritual passion.

When Christ opens and enters a man's soul, that man begins to discover what it is to be connected by a deep love to God. And how to express that deep love to his wife and his children. As he learns by God's grace to "walk in the spirit," in essence he begins to live life from the soul. His deepest desires and values are transformed. His motivations are made over. Priorities change. An old life starts to wither—a new one is resurrecting. Out of the dust and hard clay of his own weaknesses and strengths, a new-focused spiritual man emerges.

The Power of Passion

Passion is the flame that the Spirit of God lights in the soul of man. It keeps a man faithful when he is surrounded by unfaithfulness. It focuses his mind when circumstances are confusing. It brings peace to his heart when having peace doesn't make sense. It draws him on a certain path when the way is clear to no one else.

Certain men come to mind when I think of passion. For instance, Chuck Colson and his passion for prison ministry. Dr. James Dobson and his heart for families. Dr. Billy Graham and his passion for evangelism and lost souls. All of these are people with a passion in life that guides and compels them forward.

Rick Gelinas describes passion this way:

> [The] secret . . . is to have passion. Unbridled, unembarrassing, unflinching, foolish, undying passion! I am absolutely driven by what I do. It's the most important thing in my life. I am a fool for my mission, and I love being that fool! Let me explain why I am so passionate.
>
> I got into the work I do to try to "recreate" my son. He was killed by a man too stoned on cocaine to know his car had hit a little boy on a bicycle. My grief nearly killed me. Linda, my wife, and I decided to heal ourselves by dedicating our lives to helping children avoid growing up into the kind of adult who can do that. See, I don't regard what I do as work. It's a dedication, passion, and mission.[2]

At the very core of his being, every man is hungry to discover his God-given passion—the mission and focus in life for which he was created. We cannot even begin to find our reason for being—the reason God made us "a living soul"—until we escape the pride and pull of the world and find spiritual passion in our life with God.

Bottom line: When Jesus chose to paint a portrait of the soul set free, He did not give a resumé of tasks accomplished or titles achieved. He painted a picture of *virtues*—or *attitudes*—each one emerging from a heart given to God. In a powerful discourse, which we know as the Sermon on the Mount, Jesus described what the man with a soul set free looks like.

The Source of Passion

What does a man who lives life from the soul look like? What does he do? What does he sound like? What kinds of qualities and characteristics does he exhibit? What does he admit and say to the people in his life and to God?

Climbing a steep hill that overlooks the Sea of Galilee, Jesus turned to face a multitude that had followed Him. Like every one of us today, these people wanted to know what they needed to do to live a happy, fulfilled life. How they could live passionately, with purpose and inner reward.

And so Jesus addressed them in a series of statements that began: "Blessed—or *happy*—are you if . . ." And so He laid out the road to inner power and passion—a road that leads straight through the heart.

The First Attitude of a Soul Set Free: "Blessed are the poor in spirit, for theirs is the kingdom of heaven" (Matthew 5:3).

THAT'S A MAN WHO CAY SAY: "I NEED HELP!"[3]

Men struggle to admit "I need help." The Sylvester Stallone model of masculinity keeps men from admitting weakness, failure, or shortcomings. Our souls are often bombarded with cultural clichés: "Never let 'em see you sweat!" "Big boys don't cry!" "Be a self-made man!" "If you want a job done right you have to do it yourself!"

Stuart Briscoe challenges these shallow assumptions:

> Modern "macho" man in American society is not supposed to be vulnerable. According to research, the five most difficult statements for the modern man to make are (1) "I don't know"; (2) "I was wrong"; (3) "I need help"; (4) "I'm afraid"; and (5) "I'm sorry." In other words, according to the world's definition, real men do not admit to any vulnerability. And if they do, their masculinity is in question.[4]

When Jesus used the word "poor," He was describing someone who is destitute, a person who needs help—someone who knows they cannot make it on their own. Spiritual poverty occurs in the person who recognizes his own limitations and his incredible need for God's help. This kind of man says freely, "I need you, Jesus! What I am on my own is not enough. I need Your Spirit in me."

What an odd way to begin telling people how to find life's meaning! But God can only fill men who recognize how small and empty they are without Him. He can only strengthen those who realize their weaknesses. Twelve-step programs throughout the world have as their first tenet of recovery the admission of powerlessness. And long before support groups made it Step #1 of twelve, Jesus made it Step #1 of eight.

The Second Attitude of a Soul Set Free: "Blessed are those who mourn, for they will be comforted" (Matt. 5:4).

THAT'S A MAN WHO CAN SAY: "I AM SENSITIVE! I FEEL!"

The shortest verse in the Bible is also perhaps the most intriguing: *Jesus wept* (John 11:35). In the face of Christ on the pages of the New Testament we see a broad assortment of emotions. Passion poured out of his soul in many different ways: He *wept* with Mary of Bethany over her brother's death; He *burned with anger* and turned over the tables of men who had corrupted the temple with their high-priced merchandising; He was *overwhelmed with anxiety* in the Garden of Gethsemane as He anticipated His crucifixion; and He was *joyously astonished* at the great faith of a Roman centurion.

Philip Yancey challenges us to rethink the emotional side of Christ:

> The personality that emerges from the Gospels differs radically from the image of Jesus I grew up with, an image I now recognize in some of the older Hollywood films about Jesus. In those films, Jesus recites his lines evenly and without emotion. He strides through life as the one calm character among a cast of flustered extras. Nothing rattles him. He dispenses wisdom in flat, measured tones. He is, in short, the Prozac Jesus.
>
> In contrast, the Gospels present a man who has such charisma that people will sit three days straight, without food, just to hear his riveting words. He seems excitable, impulsively "moved with compassion" or "filled with pity." The Gospels reveal a range of Jesus' emotional responses: sudden sympathy for a person with leprosy, exuberance over his disciples' successes, a blast of anger at coldhearted legalists, grief over an unreceptive city, and then those awful cries of anguish in Gethsemane and on the cross. He had nearly inexhaustible patience with individuals but no patience at all with institutions and injustice.
>
> I once attended a men's movement retreat designed to help men "get in touch with their emotions" and break out of restrictive stereotypes of masculinity. As I sat in a small group, listening to other men tell of their struggles to express themselves and to experience true intimacy, I realized that Jesus lived out an ideal for masculine fulfillment that nineteen cen-

turies later still eludes most men. Three times, at least, he cried in front of his disciples. He did not hide his fears or hesitate to ask for help: "My soul is overwhelmed with sorrow to the point of death," he told them at Gethsemane; "Stay here and keep watch with me." How many strong leaders today would make themselves so vulnerable?[5]

In short, Jesus was free to live life from the soul. He freely exhibited emotion without ever compromising his masculine drive or mission—without jeopardizing His leadership.

Men today, however, tend to ignore the problems in their lives and opt to stuff their emotions, hoping that they will simply go away. Allowing ourselves to sense and feel connects us with the struggles of other people and with the difficult realities of the world. If we ignore feelings altogether because we're so fixated on our own goals and missions, we may actually miss some important work God wants us to do in service to Him and to others.

Emotions are a gift from God and they serve important functions. Emotions

- help us monitor our needs;
- provide energy for personal growth;
- make us aware of good and evil;
- provide motivation to change bad or hurtful situations;
- enhance our sensitivity to other people;
- color our expressions of worship to God;
- enrich our relationships, our marriage, and our families.

When Jesus opens the soul of a man, He does more than pour in forgiveness and the assurance of an eternity in God's presence. He begins to focus our emotions toward drives and desires that serve His kingdom and purposes. Allowing the power of your emotions to be directed by God's grace, rather than being dissipated in depression or punishing anger, is a huge step on the road to setting your soul free.

When a man is connected to God, he can *feel* on a deeper level and be more wonderfully alive than ever before. Blessed—and free from within—is the man who tastes the grace of God in all the emotions of his life, who lets them be turned into godly passion for service.

The Third Attitude of a Soul Set Free: "Blessed are the meek, for they will inherit the earth" (Matthew 5:5).

THAT'S A MAN WHO CAN SAY: "I AM STRONG, BUT I AM EASY TO LIVE WITH."

Most of us think *meek* is *weak*. But that isn't true. Meekness is a combination of *strength and humility, confidence and brokenness*. It is having the power to do good and right without causing harm—a winning combination that is rarely found and desperately needed in our boastful, pushy world.

One of the meekest men in history was John the Baptist. Josephus, a preeminent first-century Jewish historian, reported that many years after John's death, people still trembled at the thought of him when his name was mentioned! Jesus eulogized John, saying, "There has not risen anyone greater than John the Baptist" (Matthew 11:11). But when John first saw Jesus, instead of bringing attention to his own ministry accomplishments, he instructed his disciples, saying, "He [Jesus] must become greater; I must become less" (John 3:30). Such is the statement of a meek man. For the meek man sees greatness as something he must *descend* into.

So strong was John that Herod Antipas was terrified of him and his influence. And so humble was John that when asked who he was, he replied in effect, "I am nobody. I am to be heard, not seen. I am just a voice preparing the way for another."

Today men grapple for attention and recognition. After all, this is the age of the *Fortune 500*, the *25 Most Intriguing People*, the *Grammy Awards*, the *Academy Awards*, the *Emmy Awards*, and the "Top Ten" of just about everything. We live in a season of superlatives—the *greatest* athlete, the *most successful* businessman, the *best* salesman, the pastor with the *biggest* church. We want power, position, fame, and acclaim. And yet . . .

Did you ever notice that in all of the psalms David wrote he never brings our attention to his victory over Goliath? Have you observed that Paul, the greatest church-builder who ever lived, refers to himself as "the chief of sinners"? This is because these men had something most of us don't—meekness.

Meekness is not dejection; it is not insecurity. On the contrary, the meek man is strong and confident in the Lord. Experience has shown him his own weakness and need for God. With his soul set free from reliance on an army of one—himself—he bases his hope and strength on the God of heaven and earth.

A meek man knows God, but he also knows himself.

When Oscar Hammerstein was forty-six, he was a struggling composer. He had co-written with thirty different musicians and nothing he produced had truly succeeded. Down and out, despairing and dispirited, he locked arms with another unknown named Richard

Rogers. The next year they wrote *Oklahoma*, and the rest is history. He became successful beyond his wildest imagination—so successful that he decided to take out a full-page ad in *Variety* magazine.

When the readers turned to the ad that day they saw in bold print the headline: "I've done it before and I can do it again!" Then, just beneath, Hammerstein listed every single one of his failed projects.

On that day one successful man proved that his success had gone to his heart and not to his head.

The Fourth Attitude of a Soul Set Free: "Blessed are those who hunger and thirst for righteousness, for they will be filled" (Matthew 5:6).

THAT'S A MAN WHO CAN SAY: "I WANT TO KEEP ON GROWING."

It is a sad thing when a man has lost his zeal for life.

One reason many men give up on life is that they live with a narrow, self-centered focus. And after a while everything they've done to please themselves—whether in business, ministry, or hobbies—runs dry (and it always does, sooner or later). When the fire dies, life becomes cold as ashes.

Christ, however, promised men the adventure of their lives: "I have come that they may have life, and have it to the full" (John 10:10). In His Sermon on the Mount, Jesus said the ones who would be filled would be the ones who had a definite hunger and thirst for righteousness—to fulfill God's will.

That passion shows up again and again in the life of Paul the apostle, not only when preaching in the urban centers of the Greek world, but also while sitting in a dingy prison cell. The chains around his body could not contain the passion of his soul to see God's Word go forth. And life, power, faith, hope, and love poured into the letters he wrote to Christians in his day—spilling down through the ages to encourage you and me today in godly living.

Though the world eyes the Christian cynically, there is nothing at all presumptuous about aspiring to live as a righteous man. Christ gave His life that we might rise *in* our lives and become "the righteousness of God" in Christ (2 Corinthians 5:21). True, there *is* something appallingly ugly about the spirit of a man who is *self*-righteous. Self-righteousness conveys that a person thinks he has grown all there is to grow and learned all there is to know. Such a man has stopped growing because he has lost his "hunger and thirst."

But the man who stays open in heart to know more about God and His ways, and to serve others better, opens himself to more life.

The Fifth Attitude of a Soul Set Free: "Blessed are the merciful, for they will be shown mercy" (Matthew 5:7).

THAT'S A MAN WHO CAN SAY: "I CARE!"

The grace that repeatedly "moved" Jesus to reach out and help struggling souls was not only a passion: it was mercy. In the Old Testament we discover that our God is merciful and full of compassion (Psalm 116:5). In the New Testament, we see that Jesus' whole life and mission were motivated by the drive to show God's mercy to all.

Jesus Christ calls you and me to follow Him in choosing to live mercifully when it comes to the needs of others. His heart especially was drawn to those who had suffered because of sin, poverty, oppression, and weakness. So strongly did He identify with those who needed mercy that He said, "Inasmuch as ye have done it unto one of the least of these my brethren, ye have done it unto me" (Matthew 25:40, KJV).

Sometimes we can look at needy people and think we know exactly what they should do to help themselves: "If that guy would stop feeling sorry for himself and get on with life . . ." "If that woman would stop running here and there and stay home with those three kids of hers . . ." "If those parents would just come down hard on that strong-willed child . . ." We *know* what they should do.

Maybe we are right; but we can be right and also be full of judgment—rather than God's mercy.

Mercy is love that looks beyond sin and failure, weakness and foolishness. It comes alongside, lifts up, and empowers.

When a man begins to open his soul fully to God he is free to stop judging and criticizing and can thus open his soul up to others, especially those in need. Who are the people in and around your life who desperately need the mercy that God can pour through you?

The Sixth Attitude of a Soul Set Free: "Blessed are the pure in heart, for they will see God" (Matthew 5:8).

THAT'S A MAN WHO CAN SAY: "MY CONSCIENCE IS CLEAR."

The Bible calls it "conscience." One dictionary defines conscience as "the testimony and judgment of the soul which gives approval or disapproval to the acts of the will; a special activity of the intellect and emotions which enables one to distinguish between good and evil."

Paul spoke of it this way: "I strive always to keep my conscience clear before God and man" (Acts 24:16).

Our conscience is a gift from God, a built-in safety monitor. It is our opportunity to be a co-witness with God, to sit in a seat of judgment with Him to choose among options and situations that we face daily in our lives.

In the beginning, a conscience was given to every man as a kind of spiritual compass. The delicate magnet on the needle tip within that compass was carefully positioned by our Creator to draw us in the right direction, but when man sinned that magnet spun dangerously out of control. Now, as a result, "there is a way that seems right to a man, but in the end it leads to death" (Prov. 16:25).

Thank God that Jesus came to die for you and me to forgive our sins and, by His blood, to "cleanse our consciences from acts that lead to death, so that we may serve the living God" (Heb. 9:14). By the power of His surrendered-to-God Spirit in us, our spiritual compasses are being set right.

What Paul wrote to a young protégé ought to be enough to motivate us to keep our conscience pure:

> To the pure, all things are pure, but to those who are corrupted and do not believe, nothing is pure. In fact, both their minds and consciences are corrupted. They claim to know God, but by their actions they deny him. They are detestable, disobedient and unfit for doing anything good (Titus 1:15–16).

The best way to maintain a clear conscience is to live in obedience to the principles of God's Word. Not only to believe what it says but to act upon it faithfully in every aspect of our lives. In public places and in private. In worship and at work.

Free in soul is the man who is growing in faith, so his senses are becoming more sharpened to discern between good and evil (see Hebrews 5:14).

The Seventh Attitude of a Soul Set Free: "Blessed are the peacemakers, for they will be called sons of God" (Matthew 5:9).

THAT'S A MAN WHO CAN SAY: "LET ME BE YOUR FRIEND."

Dads love it when their children get along. Domestic peace and tranquillity are an optimum asset to a man's soul. Clearly, God feels the same about the way His children relate to one another:

> How good and pleasant it is when brothers live together in unity! It is like precious oil poured on the head. . . . It is as

if the dew of Hermon were falling on Mount Zion. For there the Lord bestows his blessing, even life forevermore (Psalms 133).

Peacemakers are men who have learned how to build bridges.

One of my dearest friends is a man who spent most of his life building bridges and supervising the same for the government. Ed Mason, now retired, is still building bridges. His whole life, in fact, is consumed with the conviction that God has given every man the strength and necessary tools to build bridges—bridges to God, to our wives, to our sons and daughters, to our co-workers, to our brothers, and even to our enemies.

The way a man builds bridges is by *engaging* with the people around him instead of *ignoring* them. He talks *with* people instead of *about* them or *at* them. He does more than *believe* in God, he diligently *seeks* Him. Instead of *nursing* tensions, he *confronts* them. Rather than *isolating* the people who have offended him, he openly *forgives* them and repairs what was damaged.

Holding grudges, dividing friends, taking sides—these are soul killers. But building bridges of peace brings life and deep joy.

The Eighth Attitude of a Soul Set Free: "Blessed are those who are persecuted because of righteousness, for theirs is the kingdom of heaven" (Matthew 5:10).

THAT'S A MAN WHO CAN SAY: "I WILL REJOICE EVEN IN MY DOWN TIMES."

C. S. Lewis likened God's purposeful use of difficult circumstances in our lives to walking a dog. In his book *Mere Christianity*, he states that if the dog gets its leash wrapped around a pole and tries to continue running forward, he'll only tighten the leash more and more. Both the dog and the owner are after the same objective—forward motion—but the owner must resist the dog by pulling him in the opposite direction. The owner, sharing the same intention, but understanding better than the dog where he wants to go, takes an action precisely opposite to that of the dog's will. It is in this way that God uses adversity in a man's life. We will cover this vital principle further in the next chapter.

The real challenge is controlling our attitude and emotional temperature in the face of adversity. Thomas Jefferson said, "Nothing gives one person so much advantage over another as to always remain cool and unruffled under all circumstances." Such discipline of heart takes a well-nourished soul.

James advises us to "consider it pure joy" when we "face trials of many kinds," because God is using them to "develop perseverance" and make us "mature and complete, not lacking anything" (James 1:2–4). Oswald Chambers, in his classic devotional *My Utmost for His Highest*, repeatedly refers to God as "the engineer of our circumstances." This lesson is not quickly learned. Trusting that God is in control of all our circumstances is a deep-soul attitude that, in my experience, is more readily caught than taught. Yet it lies at the foundation of the soul set free.

Pastor and author Max Lucado tells about a man who embraces this transforming attitude:

> "I have everything I need for joy!" Robert Reed said. "Amazing!" I thought. His hands are twisted and his feet are useless. He can't bathe himself. He can't feed himself. He can't brush his teeth, comb his hair, or put on his underwear. His shirts are held together by strips of Velcro. His speech drags like a worn-out audio cassette.
>
> Robert has cerebral palsy. The condition keeps him from driving a car, riding a bike, and going for a walk. But it didn't keep him from graduating from high school or attending Abilene Christian University, from which he graduated with a degree in Latin. Having cerebral palsy didn't keep him from teaching at a St. Louis Junior College or from venturing overseas on five missions trips. And Robert's disability didn't prevent him from becoming a missionary to Portugal. He moved to Lisbon, alone, in 1972. There he rented a hotel room and began studying Portuguese. He found a restaurant owner who would feed him after the rush hour and a tutor who would instruct him in the language.
>
> Then he stationed himself daily in a park, where he distributed brochures about Christ. Within six years he had led seventy people to the Lord, one of whom became his wife, Rosa.
>
> I heard Robert speak recently. I watched men carry him in his wheelchair onto the platform. I watched them lay a Bible in his lap. I watched his stiff fingers force open the pages. And I watched people in the audience wipe away tears of admiration from their faces. Robert could have asked for sympathy or pity, but he did just the opposite. He held his bent hand up in the air and boasted, "I have everything I need for joy." His shirts are held together by Velcro, but his life is held together by joy.[6]

Robert Reed had a decision to make every day: choose to complain or choose joy. The man who chooses joy has something to embrace *and* something to reject each time hardship, temptation, or annoyance confronts him. Instead of allowing his outer circumstances to control the inner temperature of his soul, he chooses to moderate his heart by actively trusting the Lord and looking to the guiding values deeply rooted in his life.

The steps of a man who is learning to walk spirit-to-Spirit with God avoid the soul-strangling temptations that arise in everyday life. Given a voice, those temptations would lead us into the kingdom of unhappiness, with laws that might read something like this:

The Laws of Unhappiness

1. Make little things bother you. Not let them, MAKE them!
2. Lose your perspective on things, and keep it lost. Don't put first things first—major on the minors.
3. Get yourself a good worry—something about which you can do nothing *but* worry.
4. Be a perfectionist: Condemn yourself and others for not achieving perfection.
5. Be right, always right, perfectly right all the time. Be the only one who is right, and be rigid about your rightness.
6. Don't trust and believe people or accept them at anything but their worst and weakest. Be suspicious. Impute ulterior motives to everyone.
7. Always compare yourself unfavorably to others. This will guarantee instant misery.
8. Take personally, with a "chip on your shoulder," everything that happens to you that you don't like.
9. Don't give yourself wholeheartedly or enthusiastically to anyone or anything.
10. Make happiness the aim of your life instead of taking life's barbs with a "bitter with the sweet" philosophy.[7]

A soul set free. In the list of characteristics we have considered, Jesus paints a vivid picture of what a man looks like who is truly free. Like a wise foreman, Jesus described what He was determined to produce in the lives of the men He called to himself. These eight qualities were the godly traits He was committed to modeling and nurturing in their souls. His words and His ways would confront, shape, and refine them until these qualities began to emerge in their attutudes, actions, and reactions. It does us good to remember that Michaelangelo's *David*, the magnificent statue, was first a very large chunk of hard rock. The final product was in the artist's eyes before it was ever hammered out in the raw material.

SOUL OPENER

Drawing Closer to God

"My soul will boast in the Lord."

Psalm 34:2

The Beatitudes paint a portrait of the kind of man Jesus can help us to become. Instead of laying out hair-splitting personality traits, He used a broad brush to capture attitudes of the soul that define a man who wants to live close to God—a righteous man. The result is growth in Christ, for these are His traits—something, via the grace of God, that's within reach of every man who is willing.

Read the eight attitudes listed below and keep them in mind as you answer the following questions:

- Which of these Christlike qualities/attitudes do you see *most* in yourself?
- Which do you see the *least*, or *not at all?*
- What man do you know who most consistently exemplifies some or all of these ideals in his daily living? What is he doing that you are not?

If you're feeling especially courageous, ask your wife or a Christian brother what his or her answers to these questions would be as they concern you. (Truth sometimes hurts initially, but it always helps ultimately.)

- "I need help!"
- "I am sensitive! I feel!"
- "I am strong, but easy to live with!"
- "I want to keep on growing."
- "I care."
- "My conscience is clear."
- "Let me be your friend."
- "I will rejoice even in my down times."

Devote some time today to asking God for strength and help to grow in your areas of weakness. Thank Him for the grace you already see at work in your life. Invite Him to confront, change, and empower you to take a few more steps of a righteous man today.

Notes

1. Richard Foster, *Celebration of Discipline*, revised edition (San Francisco: Harper and Row, 1978, 1988), p. 1.
2. Jack Canfield and Mark Victor, *The Aladdin Factor* (New York: Berkley Books, 1995), p. 142.
3. Paraphrases of the Beatitudes are borrowed from Dr. George Wood. Used by permission. ´
4. From a devotional by Stuart Briscoe in *NIV Men's Devotional Bible* (Grand Rapids, MI: Zondervan Publishing House, 1993), p. 1132.
5. Philip Yancey, *The Jesus I Never Knew* (Grand Rapids, MI: Zondervan Publishing House, 1995), p. 88.
6. Max Lucado, *The Applause of Heaven* (Waco, TX: Word Books, 1990), pp. 6–7.
7. Derived from *The Pastor's Story File* (Number 27, Vol. 3, No. 3), January 1987, p. 7.

CHAPTER FOUR

Opening a Man's Soul

"What good will it be for a man if he gains the whole world, yet forfeits his soul?"

Matthew 16:26

"All happenings, great and small, are parables whereby God speaks; . . . the art of life is to get the message."

—Malcolm Muggeridge

"If only I could persuade timid souls I meet to listen to that inner voice of the Spirit that challenges us to attempt great things for God and expect great things from God."

—Tony Campolo

Jesus never backed down from any man. Not even short-fused tempers and inflated egos got in the way of His mission. One look at the band of disciples He called to himself tells you He brought together a virtual cross section of what is weakest and worst in a man.

There was the ever-impetuous Peter, who once thought so highly of himself that he assumed the role of "prophet" and proceeded to "rebuke" Christ. There were the sons of Zebedee, James and John, whom Jesus called "Sons of Thunder"—revealing the explosive and impulsive side of their natures. Of course, there was the cynical, doubting Thomas, and the bean-counting, corrupted opportunist Judas Iscariot. And the self-proclaimed world-changer Simon the Zealot. It was a band of strong and selfish personalities that Christ called to help usher in His kingdom on the earth.

Undoubtedly there were times when at least some of these disciples thought, *I'm glad Jesus called me to help in his mission of world domination. Surely some of my skills and background—which evidently caught His attention—will serve to further His noble cause.* But what they soon discovered was that Jesus' ultimate goal was not to "utilize their noteworthy talents," but to teach them how to surrender their self-centeredness and to come alive in God. Self-actualization was not His priority; confession, repentance, and transformation were.

The Ultimate "Soul" Man

The soul of man was a major focus of Jesus' work. The most vivid description of what He anticipated for the souls of men poured out of Him one day at the Feast of Tabernacles, before throngs of followers, skeptics, and antagonists.

To set the scene, Christ had just told His dozens of followers that He would have to die. This news came as a shock. Many were overwhelmed by such news and turned away. At this same time, the Jewish leaders were hot on Jesus' trail, determined to take His life. In order to gain more followers, Jesus' own brothers urged Him to reenter Judea and do some public relations work. "No one who wants to become a public figure acts in secret," they told Him. "Since you are doing these [miracles], show yourself to the world" (John 7:4). Clearly they were more concerned that Jesus maximize His chances of celebrity status than fulfill some spiritual mission.

Jesus put aside their counsel. It was worldly and out-of-touch with God's plan. He chose to stay in Galilee and sent them on to the feast in Jerusalem. Not long after, though, He went also—as John says, "not publicly, but in secret" (John 7:10). The Scriptures tell us the community was abuzz with people asking, "Where is that man?" Widespread whispering permeated the crowds, for they all feared the threatening religious leaders. Some affirmed their belief in Jesus openly, while others rejected Him outright.

Halfway through the Feast, with the whole town wondering if Jesus would ever show up, He did. In the midst of the temple courts they found Him teaching. Amazed at His authority and insight, the Jews asked, "How did this man get such learning without having studied?" (7:14).

Jesus was apparently eager to respond to this significant question:

> My teaching is not my own. It comes from him who sent me. If anyone chooses to do God's will, he will find out

whether my teaching comes from God or whether I speak on my own. He who speaks on his own does so to gain honor for himself [i.e., *he speaks from his pride*], but he who works for the honor of the one who sent him [i.e., *from a soul committed to God*] is a man of truth; there is nothing false about him" (John 7:16–18, italics mine).

Then Jesus went for broke. Facing His opponents, He let questions fly that were aimed straight at the soul:

> Has not Moses given you the law? Yet not one of you keeps the law. Why are you trying to kill me? (7:19).

For some, the questions may have struck a bull's-eye in their conscience. For most, they came as declaration of war. With uncanny precision, Jesus' words revealed the condition of these men's souls. In an instant, it was clear that some wanted to take Jesus' life, not because they were obeying God but because they were full of anger, bitterness, and confusion. Their response:

> You are demon-possessed. . . . Who is trying to kill you? (7:20).

An Eruption of Soul

It is marvelous and challenging to me that in the face of bitter souls and murderous threats, Jesus did not retreat. He did more than face the conflict; He *engaged* it, heart and soul.

On the last day of the Feast, Jesus stood on a porch of the great temple, and shouted in a prophetic voice:

> "If anyone is thirsty, let him come to me and drink. Whoever believes in me, as the Scripture has said, streams of living water will flow from within him." By this he meant the Spirit, whom those who believed in him were later to receive (7:37–39).

At a time of ominous threats and indignant curses, Jesus did not counter with words of anger or accusation but with an *invitation*: "Come to me . . . [and] streams of living water will flow from within. . . ."

Picture yourself facing Jesus at this moment. In my mind's eye, I can see the passion on His face, hear the urgency in His voice. I sense Him looking into my soul, and this is what He sees:

First, no matter how a man looks on the outside, inwardly his soul thirsts for something deep and true and right. Jesus saw what others would miss. Standing amid a city of people bent on crowning Him or killing Him—depending on their whims or how the wind blew—Jesus saw that their weakness was a symptom of their spiritual need. While others might have seen wishy-washy, hot-and-cold souls, Jesus saw thirst.

Second, Jesus sees that I can only free my soul from its lost, stuck position by crossing a bridge called Belief. "Whoever believes in me . . ." Jesus knew that the greatest hurdle any man faces is to let himself believe. Pride is a stubborn roadblock. In order for any man to embrace the gift of God—Christ himself—he has to let go of self-sufficiency and trust as would a child.

Third, Jesus saw that the Spirit of God flows through the souls of ordinary men who are willing to love and obey. Though many wanted to snuff out His existence, He stood before them a model of what it means to live connected to God—to love and obey Him no matter what the cost. Rather than allow their anger to fuel His response, because He was surrendered to the Father's will, Jesus responded to their need. And so He offered them a whole new way of living—no longer out of the frustration of their circumstances, but from souls reconnected with God.

Inside-Out

In the eyes of the religious leaders of Jesus' day, spirituality was a matter of *appearance* and *performance.* They were into dotting *i's* and crossing *t's.* On one occasion, the Pharisees and some teachers of the law observed Jesus' disciples eating food with unwashed hands—or, in their vernacular, they were "unclean" (Mark 7:1–4). They were upset and demanded to know, "Why don't your disciples live according to the tradition of the elders? (v. 5).

Quoting the prophet Isaiah, Jesus cut to the quick and addressed the real issue:

> " 'These people honor me with their lips, but their hearts are far from me. They worship me in vain; their teachings are but rules taught by men.' You have let go of the commands of God and are holding on to the traditions of men. . . . You have a fine way of setting aside the commandments of God in order to observe your own traditions" (vv. 6–9).

Jesus revealed something essential about the soul of man. The dilemma of mankind at its deepest level does not have to do with what goes *into* the body—foods, beverages—but rather with what is allowed to *flow out* of the inner being.

> Again Jesus called the crowd to him and said, "Listen to me, everyone, and understand this. Nothing outside a man can make him 'unclean' by going into him. Rather, it is what comes out of a man that makes him 'unclean.'
> After he had left the crowd and entered the house, his disciples asked him about this parable. "Are you so dull?" he asked. "Don't you see that nothing that enters a man from the outside can make him 'unclean'? For it doesn't go into his heart [*soul*] but into his stomach, and then out of his body. . . ."
> He went on: "What comes out of a man [*out of his soul*] is what makes him 'unclean.' For from within, out of men's hearts, come evil thoughts, sexual immorality, theft, murder, adultery, greed, malice, deceit, lewdness, envy, slander, arrogance and folly. All these evils come from inside and make a man 'unclean' " (Mark 7:14–23, *italics mine*).

The greatest threat to a man is hateful or lustful thoughts that go unchecked, bitter feelings left unresolved, and ungodly attitudes that rot his soul. Suddenly, it comes clear: religious observances are not where it's at. Rather, God holds us accountable for what comes out of our heart.

The "First" Victory

Jesus knew that when a man lives life full of the Spirit of God, his own spirit becomes centered in a new, consistent, motivating will to honor God. As a result, a man is able to monitor and renew the condition of his soul—his thoughts, feelings, and desires—and to govern the use of his body in service to the purposes of God.

Victory over our own soul is the first war a man must win:

> Better a patient man than a warrior, a man who controls his temper [*i.e. governs his soul*] than one who takes a city (Proverbs 16:32, *italics mine*).

Harry S. Truman put the principle this way: "In reading the lives of great men, I found that the first victory they won was over themselves . . . self-discipline with all of them came first." Before a man can govern his world, he must by the grace of God learn how to govern himself.

Lots of us have learned how to make a good impression. Actually, it's not that hard. A nice suit. A few manners. A little consideration. A bit of generosity here and there.

Paul urged the Corinthian Christians not to consider people on the basis of how they *appear*, but to watch and observe their spirit—that is, to observe characteristics that spring from within (2 Corinthians 5:16). He also vividly described what the "rivers of living water" look like— the character qualities that flow from a heart yielded to God. To provide contrast, he juxtaposed them against his own version of a soul-contaminated man.

The soul controlled by God's Spirit: "The fruit of the Spirit is love, joy, peace, patience, kindness, goodness, faithfulness, gentleness and self-control. Against such things there is no law" (Galatians 5:22–23).

The soul controlled by man's own nature: "The acts of the sinful nature are obvious: sexual immorality, impurity and debauchery, idolatry and witchcraft; hatred, discord, jealousy, fits of rage, selfish ambition, dissensions, factions and envy; drunkenness, orgies, and the like. I warn you, as I did before, that those who live like this will not inherit the kingdom of God" (Galatians 5:19–21).

Let the River Flow

Maybe you're asking the same question I've asked: *If the fruit of the Spirit is what flows from the soul reconnected to God, then why do I see so much that is unlike Christ flowing out of me?*

Every Christian man has, at one time or another, struggled with the disparity between godliness and his own behavior. If you're like most guys, you see good attributes and bad attributes in yourself. Maybe this morning you volunteered at church or helped a friend. When you arrived back home, maybe you greeted one of your children in the driveway with a hug and a word of encouragement—only to go inside and lose your cool with your wife over something minor.

Frustrating, isn't it?

How blessed we are to have a God who watches patiently as godliness emerges in the midst of our fallenness. His power is made perfect in our weakness (2 Corinthians 12:9). As the image of Christ is being formed within us by God's Spirit, some of our old traits are quick to leave, while others are not. I am convinced that three of the most stubborn contaminants in a man's life are *duplicity, power,* and *anger.* In the next few chapters we will take a look at men who have wrestled with each of these.

But God is at work to recreate the character of Christ within us. The following principles will help you cooperate with Him in this soul-changing work every day.

---

1. The most important thing about a Christian man is that he is a "son" of God.

A couple of years ago, I found myself in a long and drawn out soul struggle. I was busy, hard at work, but felt virtually fruitless and unproductive. It was deeply important to me to be certain that I was doing God's will and doing it His way. But it seemed as if I was going about it all wrong.

Amid that conflict, I lost my voice. Not for a few weeks, but for more than a year and a half! My speech became embarrassingly broken and weak (and I was a minister in the pulpit Sunday after Sunday). As difficult as getting through those months were (and I thank God for a loving spouse and an understanding congregation), there was a deeper struggle going on within me.

Little did I know, but I had gotten back on a treadmill. I was pounding out the work and focusing on doing God's will. All the while I was taking precious little time to reflect on what God was doing within me. Why had He allowed this ailment? Was He trying to get my deeper attention? Was I really listening?

One afternoon, while away at a conference, my wife said something to me that forever changed me. As we sat in a hotel room, I confessed to her how hard it was for me to go back out and sit at a banquet and struggle just to carry on normal conversation with people. Inspired by God, I believe, she carefully and lovingly said: "Honey, I believe God wants you to know something." I invited her to continue. "He wants you to know that before you are a pastor, before you are a husband, before you are a dad . . . to Him, the most important thing about you is that you are His son and He loves you deeply." (I must confess, almost three years later, my eyes well with tears as I record this again.)

That was it! In all my doing, I had ceased to be . . . a son. God's boy. The Scripture says that we have received "the Spirit of sonship" whereby "we cry, 'Abba, Father' " (Rom. 8:15). That Aramaic term is an affectionate one. It represents the monosyllabic utterances of a baby saying for the first time, "Daddy" or "Pappa."

This passage makes it clear. God wants to be knit together, soul to soul, with His boys, with His sons. I need to relate to Him, first and foremost, as a son does to his father.

2. Christian character is not contrived in the limelight, it emerges through testing and challenge.

Faith is highly durable. As a matter of fact, it was made for tough times.

Max Lucado writes:

> The rubber of faith meets the road of reality under hardship . . . the trueness of one's belief is revealed in pain. Genuineness and character are unveiled in misfortune. Faith is at its best, not in three-piece suits on Sunday mornings or at VBS on summer days, but at hospital bedsides, cancer wards, and cemeteries. . . . Anybody can preach a sermon on a mount surrounded by daisies. But only one with a gut full of faith can live a sermon on a mountain of pain.[1]

Few pieces of writing express more clearly the way God deals with a man than these verses by Dale Martin Stone:

When God wants to drill a man,
And thrill a man,
And skill a man;
When God wants to mold a man,
To play the noblest part;
When he yearns with all his heart
To create so great and bold a man
That all the world shall be amazed,
Watch His methods, watch His ways!
How He ruthlessly perfects
Whom He royally elects:
How he hammers him and hurts him,
And with mighty blows converts him
Into trial shapes of clay which
Only God understands;
While his tortured heart is crying
And he lifts beseeching hands!
How he bends but never breaks
When his good he undertakes;
How with every purpose fuses him;
By every act induces him
To try his splendor out—
God knows what He's about.[2]

Men's souls have seldom faced tougher trials than those of a successful Chicago lawyer and Presbyterian layman who lived in the mid–1800s. Horatio Spafford was an active Christian and a close friend of the great evangelist D. L. Moody as well as other leading Christians of his day. Many are familiar with Spafford's hymn "It Is Well With My Soul." Fewer are aware of the circumstances from which it was written. Consider how God worked to form true faithfulness and unshakable peace in this man's soul:

> Some months prior to the Chicago Fire of 1871, Spafford had invested heavily in real estate on the shores of Lake Michigan, and his holdings were wiped out by this disaster. Just before this he had experienced the death of his son. Desiring a rest for his wife and four daughters as well as wishing to join and assist Moody and Sankey in one of their campaigns in Great Britain, Spafford planned a European trip for his family in 1873. In November of that year, due to unexpected last-minute business developments, he had to remain in Chicago; but he sent his wife and four daughters on ahead as scheduled on the *SS Ville du Havre*. He expected to follow them in a few days. On November 22, the ship was struck by the *Lochearn*, an English vessel, and sank within twelve minutes. Several days later, the survivors were finally landed at Cardiff, Wales, and Mrs. Spafford cabled her husband, "Saved alone." Shortly afterward, Spafford left by ship to join his bereaved wife. It is speculated that on the sea near the area where it was thought his four daughters had drowned, Spafford penned this text with words so significantly describing his own personal grief: "When sorrows like sea billows roll . . ." It is noteworthy, however, that Spafford does not dwell on the theme of life's sorrows and trials, but focuses attention in the third stanza on the redemptive work of Christ, and in the fourth verse anticipates His glorious second coming. Humanly speaking, it is amazing that one could experience such personal tragedies and sorrows as did Horatio Spafford and still be able to say with such convincing clarity, "It is well with my soul."[3]

With this man's soul struggle in mind, consider the words he wrote as he passed over the ocean waters that had taken the lives of his four little girls:

When peace, like a river, attendeth my way,
When sorrows like sea billows roll—

Whatever my lot, Thou hast taught me to say,
It is well, it is well with my soul.

Tho Satan should buffet, tho trials should come,
Let this blest assurance control,
That Christ hath regarded my helpless estate,
And has shed his own blood for my soul.

My sin—O the bliss of this glorious tho't—
My sin, not in part, but the whole,
Is nailed to the cross, and I bear it no more:
Praise the Lord, praise the Lord, O my soul!

And, Lord, haste the day
when my faith shall be sight,
The clouds be rolled back as a scroll:
The trump shall resound and the Lord shall descend,
"Even so"—it is well with my soul.

3. Our strength of soul cannot come from circumstances, but it will come as we learn to know and trust the "engineer" of our circumstances.

As we go through life we can expect to meet our own Gethsemanes, our own Calvarys, our own Resurrections. And not only once, but perhaps many times.

Paul wrote, "I have been crucified with Christ and I no longer live, but Christ lives in me. The life I live in the body, I live by faith in the Son of God, who loved me and gave himself for me" (Galatians 2:20). He also penned these passionate words: "I want to know Christ and the power of his resurrection and the fellowship of sharing in his sufferings, becoming like him in his death, and so, somehow, to attain to the resurrection from the dead" (Philippians 3:10–11).

Oswald Chambers said,

> It is adversity that makes us exhibit [Christ's] life in our mortal flesh. Is my life exhibiting the essence of the sweetness of the Son of God, or the basic irritation of "myself" that I would have apart from Him? The only thing that will enable me to enjoy adversity is the acute sense of eagerness in allowing the life of the Son of God to evidence itself in me. . . . Our circumstances are the means God uses to exhibit just how wonderfully perfect and extraordinarily pure His Son is. Discovering a new way of manifesting the Son of God should make our heart beat with renewed excitement.[4]

4. Great souls are only formed through great struggles.

No muscle ever grows strong unless it is used again and again. It is, in fact, the resistance of difficult labor that builds it and improves its capacity. Learning how to bear stress and pressure maximizes its potential. So it is with the soul. While meditation on the Word of God soothes and enhances a man's soul, it is struggle that draws out its potential.

Charles Spurgeon, the nineteenth-century pastor, was a man who was pounded by struggles many times. He insisted:

> All the troubles of a Christian do but wash him nearer Heaven; the rough winds do but hurry his passage across the straits of this life to the port of eternal peace. . . . Great hearts can only be made by great troubles. The spade of trouble digs the reservoir of comfort deeper, and makes more room for consolation.[5]

5. Every man needs a brother in spirit to challenge him in soul growth.

When Jesus wanted to reach the world with His good news, He called twelve men together and taught them not only how to preach but *how to live together as brothers.* He spoke of forgiveness, of unity, of mercy, servanthood, love, and faithfulness.

Clearly, Jesus knew that none of these men would ever reach their potential without the encouragement and support of other brothers in Christ. In a real spiritual sense, He found them alone but He left them together. Of all the principles He had embedded in their souls, this one spoke most powerfully to their attitude toward one another: "Greater love has no one than this, that he lay down his life for his friends" (John 15:13).

SOUL OPENER

Drawing Closer to God

"When I was in distress, I sought the Lord; at night I stretched out untiring hands and my soul refused to be comforted."

Psalm 77:2

"Why are you downcast, O my soul? Why so disturbed within me? Put your hope in God, for I will yet praise him, my Savior and my God."

Psalm 42:5–6

Chuck Swindoll has said, "For God to do an impossible work, he must take an impossible man and crush him." Before God can make *any* man into a man of God, He must "harness" him—not at all unlike harnessing the will of a headstrong wild stallion.

A man must first and foremost be saved *from himself.*

Take some prayerful moments to consider the following questions:

1. Has my will been reconnected with God's will? If so, in what ways?
2. What past circumstances has God used to change me? To purify my motives? To focus my life?
3. What current circumstances is God using to change me? How am I responding to that process?

Notes

1. Max Lucado, *No Wonder They Call Him the Savior* (Sisters, OR: Multnomah Press, 1986), p. 77.
2. As quoted in *Adventure in Adversity* (Wheaton, IL: Tyndale House, 1984), Paul E. Billheimer, pp. 33–34.
3. Kenneth W. Osbeck, *101 Hymn Stories* (Grand Rapids, MI: Kregel Publications, 1982), p. 127.
4. Oswald Chambers, *My Utmost for His Highest*, updated edition (Grand Rapids, MI: Discovery House Publishers, 1992), ed. by James Reimann, May 14.
5. Charles Spurgeon, *Words of Cheer for Daily Life* (Pasadena, TX: Pilgrim Publications, 1978), pp. 24, 130.

PART TWO

A Struggling Soul
(The Man God *Loses*)

CHAPTER FIVE

A Twig in the Cement

*"Man looks on the outward appearance, but the
LORD looks on the heart."*

1 Samuel 16:7

*"Character . . . is what we are when no one is looking. It is not the same
as reputation—what other people think of us. It is not the same as
success or achievement. Character is not what we have done
but who we are."*

—Bill Hybels

*"God is more concerned about our character than our comfort. His goal
is not to pamper us physically, but to perfect us spiritually.'*

—Paul W. Powell

It is in the soul that a man's life holds together—or begins to fall apart.
The soul is the well through which God's Spirit enters and flows out,
until all areas of his life are integrated. On the other hand, a man who
has not allowed God to unify all his straying passions becomes de-
tached, frustrated, and, ultimately, fragmented as a person.

Steadiness and commitment are predominant qualities in the man
whose soul is growing in character. By God's grace, this man consistently cultivates the interior aspects of his life. Like the keeper of a
spring, he daily inspects his soul-life, filtering, replenishing his inner
strength and convictions with renewed trust in God.

Compromise, on the other hand, is a main characteristic of the man
with a struggling soul. This man can be full of good intentions, but he
is like a well-framed house without a foundation. On the outside he may

seem to have it all together while on the inside he is one major storm away from total collapse. More often he changes without even noticing it, depending on who he is with.

A committed man. A compromised man. One is a man of integrity, the other is a man of two minds. One is a guy who is becoming free to be the man God is making him, the other is more often than not a carbon copy of his companions—less of an individual than he'd like to admit.

A man who lives out of a soul that is opening to God has a life that is becoming ever more integrated. He is headed toward one of a man's crowning characteristics: *integrity*.

Integrity Today

More often than not we view "integrity" as a buzz word used to evaluate political candidates, not ourselves. We critique public leaders and how they have "missed the mark"—all the while condoning our own compromises.

It seems, too often, that the sin we detest in others we overlook in ourselves. Samuel Clemens (a.k.a. Mark Twain), saw it this way:

> When I was a boy, I was walking along a street and happened to spy a cart full of watermelons. I was fond of watermelon, so I sneaked quietly up to the cart and snitched one. Then I ran into a nearby alley and sank my teeth into the melon. No sooner had I done so, however, than a strange feeling came over me. Without a moment's hesitation, I made my decision. I walked back to the cart, replaced the melon—and took a ripe one.[1]

Clemens' story—humorous in its own way—reminds me that there is something in every man that urges us to get away with whatever we can. That is, unless we make a choice to work against the tendencies born in us as natural sons of Adam.

Small Imperfections

I was in Kingston, Jamaica, with a group of Christian men digging footers for a new inner-city church. Lacking in construction experience more than anyone, I depended on the direction of my skilled co-laborers. After digging several yards of ditches for the foundation, in the sweltering tropical heat, we started to mix and pour the cement.

As I was spreading the wet mixture with a rake, a twig fell from the bank above and into the cement. Thinking nothing of it, I continued to spread the hardening substance. A second later I was startled when our crew boss shouted, "Get that twig out of there!" I obeyed the order but couldn't understand all the fuss over one little twig.

"Don't you realize that one little twig could disrupt the integrity of the whole building?" he said to my blank response.

I was intrigued and asked him to explain.

"It would make the mixture impure and create a weak point in the foundation. It probably wouldn't cause a noticeable problem right away, but in a year or so you'd see a hairline crack in the wall and then, in a few more years, the entire wall could collapse because of it. A little twig is all it would take."

The connection is worth considering.

The *American College Dictionary* defines *integrity* as "soundness of moral principle and character, uprightness; honesty; the state of being whole, entire, or undiminished; sound, unimpaired, or in perfect condition." Our word integrity is derived from the Latin word *integer*. In mathematics, an integer is "a whole number; a complete entity." So the essence of integrity is wholeness, sameness, oneness. Integrity of character, in a practical sense, includes genuinely being in private what you profess to be in public. A person of integrity is the same through and through—the "mix" is consistent. Men of integrity are those who have chosen the challenging path of character growth over the convenient path of conformity.

Warren Wiersbe said, "Two forces are at work in our world today: God is putting things together, and sin is tearing things apart."

One of the most corrupting influences we face today is *relativism*. It pushes us to stray from the path of biblical ethics. The one thing our world is the most absolute about is that "there are no absolutes." This if-it-feels-good-how-could-it-be-so-wrong? thinking has served up a generation of men who are soft on principle and spiritually bankrupt. Consequently, men today find few solid places on which to stand morally or spiritually—often because they have so few models in their lives. It has been said, "Unless we have *within* us that which is *above* us, we will succumb to that which is *around* us."

Integrity *is* indeed about being in private what we profess to be in public. Actor Robert Redford was walking one day through a hotel lobby when a woman saw him and followed him to the elevator. "Are you the real Robert Redford?" she asked with giddy excitement. As the doors of the elevator closed, he replied, "Only when I'm alone!" In a world immersed in image, success, and status, God is looking for men who live for Him not only in word but from the center of their beings.

Man of Integrity

Daniel is a prime example of a man of integrity. The Bible says he had "an extraordinary spirit."

Media men and tabloid detectives hound public figures in hopes of discovering something incriminating or at least newsworthy. In Daniel's day his fellow administrators followed him home, spied on him, "tailed him" and searched his house. The trouble was . . . they found no skeletons in his closet. No dirt under his rug. No hanky-panky. NOTHING! Daniel was a man of personal purity. They could dig all they wanted, but Daniel still came up clean. In the end, he was thrown into the lion's den. Not because he did something wrong, but because he did something right (Daniel 6:1–4).

Don't you wish we could elect someone like that to public office? Wouldn't you like to support someone like that in public ministry? Wouldn't it be great to have a guarantee that your children would turn out like that?

Daniel's integrity was not simply a part of his personality—it was the essence of his person, the fiber of his being as a man. It gave him direction as well as depth. "The integrity of the upright guides them, but the unfaithful are destroyed by their duplicity" [that is, by "twigs in the cement"] (Proverbs 11:3, bracketed comment mine).

The world around Daniel—especially King Nebuchadnezzar and the pagan Babylonians—tried to squeeze him into its mold. They offered him a heathen name, new food, and a new god to worship. But Daniel remained faithful to his God, and that's what stood him a head above the lot.

Today's pressures and temptations call for godly heroes like Daniel. And men like Job who will "[make] a covenant with [their] eyes not to look lustfully upon a girl" (Job 31:1). Men who will avoid "dishonest money" deals (Proverbs 13:11). Men who will keep the promises they make no matter what the cost (Proverbs 13:12). These times call for something quite rare—*faithful* men!

Psalm 15 could be titled the "Psalm of Solidity." In it, King David ponders the question, "Lord, who may dwell in your sanctuary? Who may live on your holy hill?" The Psalmist's questions are followed by a list of moral imperatives that describe such a person:

Someone who

- is without blame;
- does what is righteous;
- is honest;

- treats his neighbor fairly;
- hates the bad and loves the good;
- keeps his promises no matter what the cost;
- is generous.

The list of requirements is followed by the concise conclusion that "he who does these things will never be shaken." Why? Because this kind of man will not crack and crumble in an age as shaky as ours.

In his *Treasury of David*, Charles Spurgeon writes, "without integrity the best graces we have are counterfeit and therefore but glorious sins; the best worship we can perform is but hypocrisy and therefore abominable in God's sight. For uprightness is the soundness of all graces and virtues, as also of all religion and worship of God, without which they are nothing sound and worth nothing."

The Tests of Integrity

In David's public prayer, just prior to his death, he affirmed: "I know, my God, that you test the heart and are pleased with integrity" (1 Chronicles 29:17). But what types of challenges put our integrity to the test? I believe the Bible points to two.

First, there is the *test of trouble*. Proverbs 24:10 says, "If you falter in times of trouble, how small is your strength!" It is easy to boast of integrity when all is well, but when troubles come how do we fare? Like a sure foundation, it must be worked into our lives long before trouble begins. Integrity isn't a spiritual antibiotic you pop like a pill when you need it. Rather, it is spiritual food and drink with which you fill your system daily.

At forty years of age, as Ted Williams was winding down his career with the Boston Red Sox, he suffered a pinched nerve in his neck. "The thing was so bad," he later explained, "that I could hardly turn my head to look at a pitcher." For the first time in his illustrious career, Williams was batting under .300. That year he was the highest paid player in sports, making $125,000. The following year, the Red Sox mailed him the same contract.

To everyone's surprise, Williams sent the contract back with a note requesting the full pay cut allowed in its terms—a 25 percent decrease. His reason? "My feeling was that I was always treated fairly by the Red Sox when it came to contracts. I never had any problem with them about money. Now they were offering me a contract I didn't deserve. And I only wanted what I deserved."

Williams, in effect, cut his own salary by over $30,000!

Was it upright character or downright foolishness? What would you have done?

The second challenge is the *test of prosperity*. "The crucible for silver and the furnace for gold, but man is tested by the praise he receives" (Proverbs 27:21).

Several years ago, my father was working as a produce buyer for a major grocery store chain. For several weeks he was disappointed with the poor quality of fruit a certain distributor was delivering and he was on the verge of canceling their contract. Just before the boom was lowered on the fruit vendors, Dad came face-to-face with a "test of prosperity."

For years prior to this, my mom had made it known that she wanted to own a Volkswagen "bug" convertible, the most popular compact car of the '60s and '70s. Somehow, someone found out about Mom's wish, and one day a representative from the fruit distributor strolled up to Dad and handed him a set of keys. The VW bug was sitting outside and Dad had only to renew the vendor's contract to take it home and surprise Mom. What would you do?

My father said no to the compromise and, in my eyes, passed the test that day with flying colors. His superiors thought he should take the car. But Dad's decision, I will point out, was not actually made that day. It was made long before, in a heart of faith, grounded on firm convictions and a high standard of integrity.

Considering the Blessing

There is no question; the road of uprightness is paved with difficulty. It involves struggle. Sometimes a battle. Many forces work to subvert our new life in Christ. But for the man who calls upon God, He promises the strength necessary to overcome. And as a result, the life of integrity is absolutely incomparable.

Consider a few of the promises extended to the man who walks uprightly:

1. *Solidity of Character.* David said, "He whose walk is blameless and who does what is righteous . . . will never be shaken" (Psalm 15:2, 5). Integrity deals with internals—with the making of a strong spirit and a clean heart. It is the most lasting gift a child can receive from a father. Only integrity in Jesus' heart could have caused him to say, in the face of his bloodthirsty murderers, "Father, forgive them."

As weight-lifting is to muscles, so is obedience to God to the character of a man. Such a man does not fear the power of spiritual attack and troubles. As long as he maintains his integrity, nothing can shake him.

2. *Secure Footing.* "The man of integrity walks securely, but he who takes crooked paths will be found out" (Proverbs 10:9). There is a certain inbred confidence in the man of integrity. It emanates not from the ego, but from the soul. The arrogance of the unfaithful is a cheap counterfeit. A priceless peace is given to the man who disciplines himself and allows his behavior to flow from his beliefs.

3. *Succession of Righteousness.* "The righteous man leads a blameless life; blessed are his children after him" (Proverbs 20:7). By 1900, A. E. Winship had tracked down 1400 descendants of Jonathan Edwards, the famed eighteenth-century New England revivalist. Winship published a study of them in contrast to the Jukes family, a notorious clan who cost New York State $1,250,000 in welfare and prison costs. Only twenty of the 1200 Jukes descendants tracked in this study ever had gainful employment—the others were either criminals or lived on state assistance. In contrast, the Edwards lineage had contributed richly to society and to the Church.

God's blessing on the marriage and example of Jonathan and Sarah Edwards was far-reaching. By 1900, when the study was made, this family line had produced:

- 13 college presidents
- 65 professors
- 100 lawyers, and a dean of an outstanding law school
- 30 judges
- 66 physicians
- 80 holders of public office (3 U.S. senators, mayors of 3 large cities, 3 governors, a vice-president, and a U.S. treasurer
- 135 authors
- hundreds in Christian ministry
- several bank presidents.

God makes this two-edged promise: "I, the Lord your God, am a jealous God, punishing the children for the sin of the fathers to the third and fourth generation of those who hate me, but showing love to a thousand generations of those who love me and keep my commandments" (Exodus 20:5–6).

In his book *Lyrics*, Oscar Hammerstein II talks about diligence: "[Once] I saw a picture of the Statue of Liberty . . . taken from a helicopter, and it showed the top of the statue's head. I was amazed at the detail. The sculptor had done a painstaking job with the lady's coiffure, and yet he must have been pretty sure that the only eyes that would ever see this detail would be the uncritical eyes of sea gulls. He could not have dreamt that any man would ever fly over this head. He was artist enough, however, to finish off this part of the statue with as much care as he devoted to her face and her arms and the torch and everything that people can see as they sail up the bay. . . . When you are creating a work of art, or any other kind of work, finish the job perfectly. You never know when a helicopter, or some other instrument not at the moment invented, may come along and find you out."

Daniel was also diligent—and found faithful. But Scripture cries out to us: "Many a man proclaims his own loyalty, but who can find a trustworthy man?" (Proverbs 20:6).

Remember, Daniel was one of the top officials in Babylon. He had a long list of responsibilities to fulfill on the job. All the expectations! All the pressures! All the work! Yet he spent time with God daily, for we read, "Three times a day he got down on his knees and prayed . . . just as he had done before" (Daniel 6:10). He didn't turn to prayer in panic— he maintained a consistent and private prayer life—disciplined and diligent.

Downright Upright!

God laid down His absolutes in the Ten Commandments. When Jesus came with the gospel of the kingdom, He did not erase those distinct lines of law. He filled them in with the Technicolor of His life and example. He came to fulfill the Law—to get it deep within our hearts . . . to make a way for us to live it out from the soul.

Jeremiah foresaw a day when men would be transformed from the inside out: "The day will come," says the LORD, "when I will make a new covenant . . . I will put my laws in their minds, and I will write them on their hearts. I will be their God, and they will be my people. . ." (Jeremiah 31:31-33 NLT).

Jesus pointed out that murder was not only an action, but first and foremost an attitude of the heart. Our anger and hatred are the real seeds of sin (Matthew 5:21-22). This kind of standard is beyond anything that we can ever achieve ourselves. Humanly speaking, integrity evades us and God's law is unattainable in our sinful state. The gospel of Jesus Christ, however, offers not only forgiveness of sins but power to grow in godliness—every day.

A Faithful Man's Two Best Friends

In his Gospel, John reported that Jesus was filled with two things: "grace and truth" (John 1:14). These are the two most important sources of spiritual fuel in a man's life. Every one of us needs heavy doses of grace to overcome our challenges. Only Christ can put grace within us. The Bible says that grace is His to give to every man (Ephesians 4:7).

When a soul-stuck man encounters the Christ he meets the One who on the cross was made "to be sin for us, so that in him we might become the righteousness of God" (2 Corinthians 5:21). Then his life is touched by grace. Suddenly new desires—godly ones—begin to emerge within his soul. Those desires do not automatically erase our old sinful desires. They do help him win in the spiritual battle that vies for the ultimate influence in our lives. Grace is the God-given empowerment that sets a man free to be all that God intended.

Grace will fill those areas where truth has carved out a place for God to work. In order to live life from the soul, a man must not only face the truth about himself, he must embrace it. This is the most courageous step a man will ever take—*facing the truth about himself, his sins, his failures, his vulnerabilities.* Most of us are experts at avoiding the truth about ourselves.

Christ consistently brought men to the place of truth so that He might release His grace more fully within them. "You will know the truth, and the truth will set you free" (John 8:32). He confronted Peter over his stubbornness. He faced down the Pharisees over their attitudes of self-righteousness. He challenged James and John concerning their anger.

While some would resist the confrontations of Christ, the wise man understands that the deep-digging spade of truth opens up a soul to the fullness of God's grace and Spirit. Integrity is cultivated by truth and preserved by grace.

Enemies of Integrity

The Bible cites the enemies of a man of God as the "world," the "flesh," and the "devil." R. C. Sproul defines those respectively as a fallen planet ("world"), fallen man ("the flesh") and fallen angels ("the devil"). In the next chapters we will look at two of the greatest temptations that men face: the "biggies" are anger and hunger for power. We need to face these foes, and learn how living life from the soul can lead a man to overcome and to walk in integrity in all his ways.

Soul Openers

Inspecting Your Soul

Self-confrontation is a habit of the man of character. More often then not, truth is uncomfortable and hard to face. And yet, it works hand-in-hand with the grace God wants to release in our lives.

Ask yourself the following questions. Consider them deeply. If you are feeling especially courageous, ask a friend to answer them about you:

1. Do I pay my debts faithfully and promptly?

2. Which is more important to me, getting the best of whatever situation I am in or dealing fairly?

3. In the following areas and in light of God's standards, am I committed or compromising?

- In my marriage relationship
- As a father
- At business, and on the job
- As a friend
- On my taxes

4. Can I be trusted

- with an expense account
- with alone hours in my day
- with projects, assignments, and responsibilities?

5. Are my words behind peoples' backs more often positive or negative?

6. Do I admit my weaknesses, struggles, and problems to others in my life regularly?

7. To whom am I accountable? Is that submission wholehearted or halfhearted?

A Prayer for Integrity

Heavenly Father, You are the one true God, perfect in every way. Thank You that amid a world full of hypocrisy and duplicity, You are always the same. You never change. It brings me great security, as a follower of Christ, to know that Your character does not change with the wind. Your love for me is constant. You will never leave me or turn Your back on me. What strength and certainty Your consistent character brings to my prayers and faith.

Forgive me, Lord, for the times when I have been double-minded and hypocritical. For the times I have made promises and not kept them. For the religious "masks" I have worn and the times I have talked the talk, but not walked the walk.

Make me whole. Make me pure-hearted. Make me a man of integrity and honesty. Build into my heart, mind, and life, character that cannot be shaken. Help me to walk with single-hearted devotion in the path you have placed before me. In Jesus' name. Amen.

Notes

1. Elizabeth Dodds, *Marriage to a Difficult Man: The Uncommon Union of Jonathan and Sarah Edwards* (Philadelphia: Westminster Press, 1971), pp. 37–38.

CHAPTER SIX

The Fire in Your Soul

"Be angry but do not sin; do not let the sun go down on your anger."

Ephesians 4:26, RSV

"Anyone can become angry—that is easy. But to be angry with the right person, to the right degree, at the right time, for the right purpose, and in the right way—this is not easy."

—Aristotle

Several years ago, I encountered true anger. I mean anger personified. Red-faced, bust-a-blood-vessel anger.

My wife, Pam, and I had been counseled that three to four months before the birth of your first baby is "prime time" for a weekend getaway. It was fall, and we took off to discover some vacation spots in central Pennsylvania and enjoy the changing mountain foliage. Our married life was about to change, and we needed a few days to simply be together.

Being on a small budget, we selected an inexpensive motel tucked into the rolling countryside. The manager—a smiling blond-headed hulk who told us he was an ex-professional hockey player—happily showed us to our room. We kicked off our shoes, all indicators pointing to a wonderful weekend ahead.

The *we're-on-vacation* feeling was still strong the next morning. In the interest of saving a few bucks, we fixed a light breakfast—some warmed-up Danish and brown-and-serve sausages—in a portable skillet. The phone rang, and it was our friendly hockey player host with a special request.

Another couple had just checked in. Come to find out, they'd spent their honeymoon in the very room we were in. They'd been hoping to have the same room again. Would it be inconvenient for us to move to the room right next-door? Happy to help them out, we consented.

Just settling into our new room, the phone rang again. I guessed it was the manager, and I was anticipating a *thank-you*.

Instead, the phone fairly exploded. "You were cooking in that room, weren't you?" he shouted in my ear. "Didn't you see the sign in the office last night?"

I apologized, and said we obviously had missed the sign. We were sorry.

"I can't believe you!" he ranted. "You two are pigs! You're absolute pigs! I don't want you in my place! Pack up right now and get out of here . . . just get out!"

My attempts to calm him down, to apologize and to reason, made no difference. And the more he rejected my calm replies, the more something began to fray in me. In a minute my blood began to boil as adrenaline shot through my veins. Ferocious fantasies filled my mind—like driving my car through his office wall!

Thankfully, I was able to draw on something stronger inside and bring the boil down to a simmer. I was able to recognize that the true inner battle was between what my impulses were dictating and what God was trying to teach me.

We will never forget the feelings we had as we packed our car—humiliation, rejection, anger, frustration, and deep embarrassment. All day, while touring the area, a dismal cloud hung over us. We kept commenting to each other, "Don't you feel like people are looking at us? Like they know we did something that got us into trouble?"

Angry, reckless words had struck deep, crushing our dream weekend. Instead of feeling refreshed, our souls felt scorched.

I vowed then that I would never unleash destructive, soul-scorching anger on anyone. On a few previous occasions, I'd been known to.

And today—though I've come a few more steps in terms of self-control—I'm aware of the force that's lurking inside me. A force that can be used to help, to heal, or to hurt.

A force that I, as a man, need to submit constantly to the control and direction of God.

Three Strikes

Moses was a man with quite a track record of anger.

It seems he wrestled with anger for years until it got the best of him.

When something angered him, his impulse was to strike. Consider Moses' response to three genuinely provoking events.

Strike One: As a young man (Exodus 2:11–15) he saw an Egyptian beating a fellow Hebrew. Enraged by the offense, Moses beat the Egyptian to death and "hid him in the sand." But when the sand could not conceal his crime, Moses fled the country for his life in fear of Pharaoh's punishment (Acts 7:23–29). He not only lost his temper, he lost his home.

Strike Two: Years later, God got hold of Moses' life—but that did not instantly change the character of the man.

The drawn-out task of convincing Pharaoh to let the Hebrew children go tested Moses' patience. Every time Pharaoh rejected his plea, Moses' springs were wound tighter and tighter. Finally, after Moses' tenth round with the ruler, the spring let loose. The Bible says, "then Moses, hot with anger, left Pharaoh" (Exodus 11:8).

Strike Three: Moses was blessed with the high privilege of carrying the stone tablets inscribed with the Ten Commandments by God himself down from Mount Sinai to present to Israel. After a time of sheer glory, this new leader found his people breaking the very commandments he held in his hands. Seeing the Hebrews dancing around an idol—a golden calf—was more than Moses' temper could bear.

Rather than confronting the nation with the newly revealed truth—in righteous anger—"he threw the tablets out of his hands, breaking them to pieces at the foot of the mountain. And he took the calf they had made and burned it in the fire; then he ground it to powder, scattered it on the water, and made the Israelites drink it" (Exodus 32:19–20). We never read that God approved of Moses' punishing behavior. On the contrary, the text implies that God instructed Moses to obtain a second copy of the list of laws by inscribing this one *himself* (Exodus 34:27–28).

Anger took hold of Moses, body and soul. He was driven by anger *still.* And anger would be Moses' greatest source of frustration for much of the rest of his life.

Soul Storms

Most of us can quickly identify with the honest confessions of men who feel more controlled by their own inner drives, aggressions, and frustrations than they do *in control* of them. Many are the men who engage in frequent "wrestling matches" with unspoken difficulties, shortcomings, insecurities, fears, and compulsions that tend to frustrate them inwardly. And yet, social mores often dictate a message that makes the atmosphere anything but conducive for men to even speak of these struggles, much less begin to deal with them.

Consider one father's struggle with his own anger:

> I am yelling at the top of my lungs at three little girls lying still and terrified in their beds. Like a referee in a lopsided boxing match, my wife is trying to pull me away, but I am in the grip of a fury I am unwilling to relinquish. "And if you don't get to sleep right now," I shout, "there are going to be consequences you're not going to like."
>
> With that vague but ominous threat, I slam the door so hard that I hear plaster falling behind the walls. I throw myself on my own bed, out of breath, pulse jackhammering in my temples, throat bruised and burning, a growing tide of remorse and revulsion rising within. From the children's room, howls descend into sobs and then sniffling whimpers as my wife murmurs a lullaby of explanations: "Daddy loves you very much," I hear Kathy tell them—a bedtime story in which I appear as a monster whose true, kinder side is obscured by fatigue and worry. "He's just tired, and he wants you to go to sleep. No, you're right, he shouldn't lose his temper, but sometimes parents get upset, and they do things they shouldn't."
>
> I love my kids, but I have left my handprint, a faint blush, on the back of their thighs when I've spanked them. I have seen them recoil from me in terror.
>
> At the office, I'm friendly, easygoing, generally considered a nice guy. It's only at home that I display this vein-popping, larynx-scraping rage. It's not just that I never show this secret, ugly side of my personality to others; I don't even seem to feel it in any other sphere of my life. Why must loved ones bear the brunt of anger?[1]

The Anatomy of Anger

For many men, anger is their master. You don't rule *it*—*it* rules you. According to Dr. James Dobson, anger can take a person over emotionally *and* physically. When we get angry, an automatic warning system is set off. Maybe it's a set of words, a certain tone, an unexpected event that triggers it. Even a familiar smell can be perceived as threatening. Instantly, the body marshals its defenses. The bloodstream rushes a fresh explosion of adrenaline to the heart, quickening the pulse, raising the blood pressure, dilating the eyes (enhancing peripheral vision), and pumping energy into the muscles. The body is propelled into an *alarm-reaction state*.

No, we cannot stop our body from experiencing its fight-or-flight response. But we can *take charge* of that strike-out impulse—overruling it with better, healthier, more productive responses, *godly responses* that get at spiritual issues. That's why Solomon wisely observed, "Better a patient man than a warrior, a man who controls his temper than one who takes a city" (Proverbs 16:32).

How do we begin to overrule—or more rightly, *rule over*—our inner man? We can begin with a little self-knowledge.

Psychologists concur after repeated studies on human behavior that there are five levels of intensity to this emotion. The first stage of anger is *irritation*, characterized by a feeling of uncertainty or uneasiness due to some unpleasant disturbance. *Indignation* is the second stage, in which we interpret a word or action as unreasonable, unfair, or threatening. When anger reaches the next level—*wrath*—it fuels the system with a boiling desire to avenge or defend oneself. It is at this stage that anger must be expressed in some way. Unless you direct your wrath into something productive, *fury* is the fourth stage, characterized by violent actions and words. The highest level of anger is *rage*. Once you've allowed your anger to spike this high, it can result in blind brutality—even a temporary loss of sanity.

Four Strikes . . . You're Out!

God gave Moses a lot of grace. He continued to choose and use Moses despite his uncontrolled anger. But there came a point when Moses' lack of ability to govern himself was going to affect a whole nation. Because he had stepped into a role of godly leadership he was a model for literally millions of people.

Whether you are a leader in the church, industry, or your home, God wants you to demonstrate the manly art of letting God direct your anger into *healthy, profitable change*. He does not want us to dissipate it internally in frustration and depression, or externally in harming others physically or verbally. If we allow Him to work in us, He will harness our anger to His purposes and transform it into a new kind of drive that is productive rather than destructive.

Moses paid a high price when he resisted surrendering the force of his anger to God.

Early in Israel's journey out of Egypt the people became thirsty. They complained to Moses and began to blame him. Tired and desperate, Moses called on the Lord, who responded, "Walk on ahead of the people. Take with you some of the elders of Israel and take in your hand the staff with which you struck the Nile, and go. I will stand there before you by the rock at Horeb. Strike the rock, and water will come out of it for the people to drink" (Exodus 17:5–6). Obediently, Moses struck the rock and the water flowed. Interestingly, Moses named that sacred spot *Massah*, which means "testing," and *Meribah*, which means "quarreling." Evidently, Moses saw the people's quarreling as a test of his own soul.

Farther along the journey, surrounded by desert heat, the Israelites again began to complain—more loudly than before: "Why did you bring the Lord's community into this desert, that we and our livestock should die here? Why did you bring us up out of Egypt to this terrible place? It has no grain or figs, grapevines or pomegranates. And there is no water to drink!" (Numbers 20:4–5).

Can you feel the irritant that poured into Moses' soul? He had heard it all before. Like a dripping faucet. And after all he'd gone through for them. . . . *Irritation* became *indignation*, then *wrath*. . . .

The pressure was on. The desert was hot. The journey, long. The vision of a promised land that prompted this expedition, worn thin by the weariness of it all. Moses had left everything to help this motley bunch. He had given of himself until he had nothing left to give, but now what did they want? They wanted more . . . still more. Water. They wanted, they expected, they insisted upon water. Their not having it was *his* fault. Their obtaining it, *his* responsibility.

It is important to remember here that God was training Moses to lead Israel *in obedience to Him*. A leader has to lead not only with his words but with his life. Keep that in mind as you view what happened next.

Moses called on the Lord to meet the people's need for water. A cloud of glory enveloped him, and God spoke clear, specific words of instruction: "Take the staff, and you and your brother Aaron gather the assembly together. Speak to that rock before their eyes and it will pour out its water. You will bring water out of the rock for the community so they and their livestock can drink" (20:8).

Before, God told Moses to *strike* the rock. Now he was only to *speak*, and the water would pour out.

Imagine the honor to God if Moses had merely said the word—and water gushed from stone. Imagine how the people would have respected God as Maker of heaven and earth, Supplier of their needs, Comforter to their weary souls and bodies. But it was not to be.

"So Moses took the staff from the Lord's presence, just as he commanded him. He and Aaron gathered the assembly together in front of the rock . . ." (20:9–10). Yes, Moses set out to obey—but on the way to obedience, his temper took over. He let Israel's file of complaints push him over the edge. Instead of focusing his drive and force into doing God's explicit will, he exploded. "Moses said to them, 'Listen, you rebels, must we bring you water out of this rock?' Then Moses raised his arm and struck the rock twice with his staff. Water gushed out, and the community and their livestock drank" (20:10–11).

Notice Moses struck the rock not once, but twice. Anger rarely settles for one blow or one insult.

Tragically, Moses' outraged venting of anger spoiled God's miracle— and it destroyed Moses' chance of leading the people into the Promised Land. The Lord told Moses: "Because you did not trust in me enough to honor me as holy in the sight of the Israelites, you will not bring this community into the land I give them" (20:12).

What's a Man to Do With His Anger?

Gordon MacDonald urges men to face the fires within:

> When we refuse to acknowledge our anger, it may ultimately rise up and betray us, laying the spiritual groundwork for bad choices, rebellious attitudes, patterns of resentment that neutralize us.
>
> I was taught from a score of sources that a Christian never becomes angry. So the rule by which I lived was to never show or admit to anger. What I did not know, was that the anger was, nevertheless, there. It was deep in the archives, festering, seething, whether or not I chose to acknowledge it and name it.
>
> Since the anger could not express itself in expected ways—sharp words, a raised voice, intense activity—it found other ways to get out. I discovered to my embarrassment that I'd acquired a withering glare. My facil expression said as much as words could ever had said. Sometimes in anger, I withdrew into silence and punished the other person by leaving her without a clue about what was wrong. I showed irritation at safe objects: the dog, an errant driver in traffic, a person on television—someone who would never know of my anger or ever fight back.

What I and others have had to learn how to say is, "I am very angry about this. And this is why . . ."

You are not unwise to stop with reasonable frequency and ask yourself, *What is the dominant feeling within me at this moment? Why is the enthusiasm I had this morning gone this afternoon? What troubles me about this decision? This person? What's at the root of my excitement, my impatience, my sense of being drawn to this or that person? What's behind the tightness in my stomach?*[2]

Remember, dads: Grown-up anger doesn't overcome a child's anger. You can't build character in your kids by outshouting them. They need your strength of spirit and firm direction. "In quietness and trust is your strength" (Isaiah 30:15).

Remember, managers: Angry blasts don't breed creativity or enhance productivity. Anger in the workplace stirs up resentment. Employees run best on the fuel of visionary leadership, clear expectations, strong and fair accountability . . . and space to grow.

Remember, husbands: Anger stored up will not only ruin a moment or a day—it may break up your marriage. Learning to love each other enough to tell each other the truth in kindness gives a marriage something to grow on. Points of anger, feelings of resentment, and roots of bitterness don't go away or heal themselves. They shut down growth. They are like a cancer in a marriage.

For a moment or two Moses probably felt relief at blowing off some steam. But for a lifetime he would live with the consequences of his actions. Moses, born into a royal environment, died in the wilderness—not in the Promised Land. "Because . . . you broke faith with me in the presence of the Israelites at the waters of Meribah . . . and because you did not uphold my holiness . . . you will not enter the land . . ." (Deuteronomy 32:51).

Soul Opener

Drawing Closer to God

"When anxiety was great within me, your consolation brought joy to my soul."

Psalm 94:19

We can learn today from Moses' hard lesson. Anger need not ruin our lives, our family relationships, our effectiveness for God. We can learn to allow God to direct the inner forces of our soul. If this story of Moses' failure has pricked your conscience, don't give up. You can change!

Devote some prayerful moments today to considering the following questions. Ask God to shine the light of His Word into your soul:

1. What kinds of things regularly make you angry?
2. How do you generally release your anger?
3. From what source(s) do you think your anger ultimately springs?
4. What people in your life are most often the brunt of your anger?
5. How does anger affect your marriage? Your parenting? Your friendships? Your work?

We tend to become angry when we feel we are losing control. We tend to become anxious when things don't go our way. In both situations we are threatened.

When you feel angry or anxious, pray. Consider the following verse, and then take some time to pray for strength:

Do not be anxious about anything, but in everything, by prayer and petition, with thanksgiving, present your requests to God. And the peace of God, which transcends all understanding, will guard your hearts and your minds in Christ Jesus (Philippians 4:6–7).

Prayerfulness and *thankfulness* characterize a godly man. Rather than being anxious, his soul is in communication with God, and he is under His direction.

Don't let anger master you or direct your life. Seek God's help today—and let Him redirect the fire in your soul to His good ends.

Notes
1. Christopher Scanlan, "A Father Confronts His Rage" (*The Boston Globe* magazine [March 5, 1995]), p.14.
2. Gordon MacDonald, *When Men Think Private Thoughts*, (Nashville, Tenn.: Thomas Nelson Publishers, 1996), p. 92.

CHAPTER SEVEN

The Ultimate Power Tool

" 'Not by might nor by power, but by my Spirit,' says the Lord Almighty."

Zechariah 4:6

"Nearly all men can stand adversity, but if you want to test a man's character, give him power."

—Abraham Lincoln

"Power is of two kinds. One is obtained by fear of punishment and the other by the art of love. Power based on love is a thousand times more effective and permanent than the one derived by fear of punishment.[1]

—Mohandas Ghandi

Home Improvement has been one of the most highly rated sitcoms in America. It's star, the overconfident Tim "The Tool Man" Taylor, is known for his insatiable passion for an arsenal of assorted *Binford* power gadgets. Just the sound of a power saw, the roar of a lawn mower, or the force of a jackhammer can cause him to lose touch with reason and make stupid decisions—like ripping out a whole wall of his home as an excuse to use some newer, better power tool.

To Tim, tools are power and power is everything. Consistently, though, his use of power gets a bit carried away, and what ultimately emerges is a clear display of personal idiosyncrasy or weakness. Maybe the reason we laugh is that we see how much like Tim we are—how often we overdo it and some strength becomes our greatest weakness. Even our downfall.

Power. Our culture is obsessed with it. Our lives, our homes, and, yes, even our churches are vulnerable to its misuse. Just think for a moment about how much the concept of power permeates our lives: power lunches, power ties, power plays, power moves, power books, power tools, power psychology, self-empowerment . . . Power Rangers. The exaltation of power fills our offices, businesses, and bookshelves. Power is big business.

The Love of Power

Napoleon wrote: "I love power. But it is as an artist that I love it. I love it as a musician loves his violin, to draw out its sounds and chords and harmonies. I love it as an artist." Nietzsche was suspicious of the Napoleons in his world, saying, "I have found power where people do not look for it, in simple, gentle, and obliging men without the least desire to domineer—and conversely the inclination to domineer has often appeared to me as a sign of inner weakness."

Others throughout history have been less enchanted with power. Lord Acton is oft-quoted as saying, "Power tends to corrupt and absolute power corrupts absolutely." Erich Fromm asserted, "The lust for power is not rooted in strength but in weakness." James F. Byrnes warns, "Power intoxicates men. When a man is intoxicated by alcohol he can recover, but when intoxicated by power he seldom recovers."

Former British Prime Minister Margaret Thatcher puts it poignantly: "Being in power is like being a lady. If you have to tell people you are, you aren't."

Husbands and wives often struggle with each other for power, children strive to pry themselves free from their parents' power, and brothers and sisters contend for it. On our jobs, many employers use force and fear tactics to compel employees, while employees pour their energies into forming unions to force change upon employers. Power permeates our culture politically, socially, racially, sexually, and financially.

In Jesus' day power was a central issue as well. The primary threat to the Jewish people was Rome and its brutish armed forces. The Romans preferred to view their own influence as "progress." The Pharisees perceived power as the means to legislate righteousness among the populace, using threats and judgment to compel them to obey tedious laws and traditions. The Zealots, tired of religious talk, were determined to fight fire with fire in the name of God—to overpower the "power brokers" of their day with the sword.

Jesus issued a warning to the Pharisees about their love of power and prestige: "Woe to you Pharisees, because you love the most important seats in the synagogues and greetings in the marketplaces" (Luke 11:43). Then He issued a challenge to the men who followed Him: "Whoever wants to become great among you must be your servant" (Matthew 20:26).

The Power of Love

When Christ confronted a society obsessed with power, He used something even more powerful: *love.*

This was not your Valentine's Day kind of sentimental love. He spoke of *agape*—a force of love that so powerfully touched and changed the heart of one zealot—the apostle John—that his nickname changed from "Son of Thunder" to "John the Beloved."

It was the transformed John who wrote about the new power he'd experienced:

> God is love. Whoever lives in love lives in God, and God in him. . . . There is no fear in love. But perfect love drives out fear, because fear has to do with punishment. The one who fears is not made perfect in love (1 John 4:16, 18).

God is love! One of the shortest sentences in the Bible—sweeping in its meaning and importance. God is *love.* It is as if *God* and *love* are interchangeable.

John the Beloved invites us to get to know God by getting to know love. To understand love by getting to know God.

Power was an essential part of Jesus' earthly ministry. Yet Jesus displayed His power only when it had the purpose of love connected to it. His healings were demonstrations of love—administered one-on-one, not *en masse.* When He multiplied the loaves and the fishes, His love saw 5,000 hungry people. And when the crowds wanted to make Him king, lavish Him with luxuries, and obey His whims—eternal Love saw the need of their souls. Then He went to the cross to save them.

If You're So Great . . .

The Pharisees were incredibly jealous of the power and attraction of Jesus. Repeatedly they asked Him to show them a sign of His power. Jesus responded, "A wicked and adulterous generation looks for a miraculous sign [of power]" (see Matthew 16:1–4, brackets mine).

It was not the first time Jesus had been tempted to prove himself by using power. He recognized the force behind the words. In essence, the Pharisees were saying, "Power and might is the only thing we serve. Prove you are from God by using your power."

Yes, Jesus knew the voice. In the wilderness, the devil had come forward, saying in effect, "Show me the power!" Consider the three blows Satan targeted at Jesus, and how He countered them.

When Jesus was weary, after a long period of fasting and prayer, the Enemy suggested, "If you are the Son of God, tell these stones to become bread" (Matthew 4:3).

In essence, Jesus responded, "Watch the love of a heart that more deeply craves the Father's words than bread" (author's paraphrase of v. 4).

Then, taking Jesus to the highest point of the temple, the devil urged Him, "Throw yourself down. . . . He will command his angels concerning you" (Matthew 4:6).

Jesus said something like, "Watch the love that refuses to play games with God!" (paraphrase of v. 7).

Finally, the Tempter ran the most panoramic and descriptive "video" of all the world's goodies and solicited, "All this I will give you . . . if you will bow down and worship me" (4:9).

Jesus retorted, "Watch the love that will not break faith with my Father. There is no one else a man should worship but God and God alone!" (paraphrase of v. 10).

That kind of power—the power of love—was too tough for even Satan to destroy.

If you are shaking your head and saying, "I don't think I can ever have that kind of powerful love," don't worry. It took a long time for Jesus' disciples to grab it, too. The world's power offerings kept them from seeing His love as the most powerful force on earth.

Consider the time Jesus attended a dinner given in His honor at the home of Lazarus, the man whom He'd raised from the dead. As Jesus and Lazarus were being served a meal, a woman came in with her most precious personal resource—a bottle of perfume worth a year's salary—and poured it on Jesus' feet, wiping them with her hair. Jesus was deeply moved. But Judas was incensed, saying, "What a waste!" One event—two views. The difference was that Judas saw the power of money. Jesus saw the power of love.

At Jesus' arrest, Peter drew his sword and lunged toward the blood-thirsty horde, striking off the ear of the high priest's servant. Jesus rebuked him. "Put your sword in its place, for all who take the sword will perish by the sword. Or do you think that I cannot now pray to My Father, and He will provide Me with more than twelve legions of angels? How then could the Scriptures be fulfilled, that it must happen thus?" (Matthew 26:52–54). The message was clear. Jesus had easy access to power, but a greater purpose and vision kept Him focused and controlled. It was the vision and purpose of saving lost souls through the redeeming power of His shed blood. Peter saw the power of anger and physical force. Jesus saw the power of laying down one's own body to do God's will—the ultimate power of love.

The Price of Power

Tony Campolo writes, "A craving for power interferes with love and destroys personal relationships. The desire to be powerful interferes with the possibility of our being real Christians. . . . Salvation lies in being surrendered to God, serving others, and giving up all attempts to be powerful."[2]

Campolo's words hit a bit too close to home for me.

Early on in our courtship a particular "power issue" began to interfere. It's laughable to me now, but in my early twenties it was no laughing matter. You see, Pam has always been an extrovert, and I was, at that time, quite the introvert. People were instantly drawn to her, and she had the ability to make them laugh, put them at ease, and give them valuable advice. These qualities had drawn me to Pam, but before long I saw them as a threat.

One evening, as we left a casual gathering with a group of friends, I felt the need to reestablish my dominance—and I attacked. "You talked more than anyone!" (What I really meant was, *I didn't quite know what to say or when to say it.*) "You told too many jokes!" (I meant, *I wish I could tell them as effectively as you.*) "Why don't you just back off and let someone else get a word in edgewise?" (*I envy your communication skills.*)

My words almost killed something within Pam's soul. Pam's vibrant personality and sensitive social skills were a gift from God meant to draw this hermit out of his shell. I had grown to resent something God was calling me to embrace. The need for control said, *View these differences as a threat.* Love said, *View them as a blessing.*

In retrospect, my problem was not with Pam—it was with my own insecurity and the need for power. You see, most of us men are not going to pull off corporate takeovers, but when our power need is not surrendered to God, we *will* try to take over something or someone—in an unhealthy attempt to feel stronger than we need to feel.

The Ultimate Power Tool

If the scene at the Last Supper had been written according to the disciples, it would have looked more like a *coup* attempt than a prayer gathering. After all, the plot had thickened and the heat was on because the Jewish officials and the Pharisees were moving in for the kill. The disciples' lives were in greater peril than ever before. If they ever needed the power that this revolutionary teacher had at His fingertips, they needed it now. What would His strategy be? When would Jesus' miracles shift from opening blind eyes to gouging out Roman eyes? How long before Jesus would mount his rightful throne and reestablish David's line?—with His loyal disciples powerfully at His side, of course.

And so they waited eagerly in the Upper Room for Jesus to roll out the battle plans and, perhaps, brandish a sword. That was when Jesus unveiled His secret weapons. His power tools of choice.

As they all watched, Jesus picked up a towel and a basin of water. Then He made His way around the table, washing their feet!

Washing Peter's feet, despite his impulsiveness.

Washing Thomas' feet, despite his doubts.

Washing James' feet, despite his brashness.

Even washing Judas' feet, despite his betrayal.

And the real "power tool" Jesus so freely demonstrated that night drilled right through the stony walls around these men's hearts. It went to the core of their prideful masculinity. He said, with every fiber of His being, *When you are tempted to use power for your own selfish ends—give yourself to God to become a servant of His great, loving purposes.*

Our lives are constantly filled with opportunities to act either with power or with love. Moment by moment, every one of us must decide what will motivate our actions, reactions, and responses—whether we'll live out of our shallow ego-needs or out of a soul surrendered to God.

These moments occur when your wife reminds you its your turn to change the diapers; when the kids spill their milk at the dinner table (for the third time in one night); when your oldest son has borrowed the tool you need and did not put it back where it belongs. It happens when your authority is questioned, your will is challenged, and your plans are rearranged.

Power or love. Force or influence.

At home, the choice we make is either to be *master* or *father*. On the job, the decision may be whether to be *boss* or *leader*.

Jesus chose to love *and* to lead. He knew that wielding a weapon could pierce the flesh, but washing feet could open the soul.

Consider the following list of contrasts:

BOSSES VS. LEADERS

A *boss* creates fear	A *leader* creates confidence
*Boss*ism creates resentment	*Leader*ship breeds enthusiasm
A *boss* says "I"	A *leader* says "we"
A *boss* fixes blame	A *leader* fixes mistakes
A *boss* knows how	A *leader* shows how
*Boss*ism makes work a drudgery	*Leader*ship makes work interesting
A *boss* relies on authority	A *leader* relies on cooperation
A *boss* drives	A *leader* leads

The pivotal event of Jesus' life and ministry was choosing the cross. What could have possibly made Him any more power*less* than submitting to an execution of the most humiliating sort?

And yet, the cross *was* a power act. For by going to the cross, He said in effect: *If you want to call yourself by my name—a Christian, a follower of Jesus—you also must lay aside your own will—power in all its disguises—and become a servant to the people around you in the place my Father has put you.*

A Serious Warning

Jesus gave us a clear warning in His Sermon on the Mount: "Not everyone who says to me, 'Lord, Lord,' will enter the kingdom of heaven, but only he who does the will of my Father who is in heaven. Many will say to me on that day, 'Lord, Lord, did we not prophesy in your name, and in your name drive out demons and perform many miracles?' Then I will tell them plainly, 'I never knew you. Away from me, you evildoers!' " (Matthew 7:21–23).

Oh yes, people admire us for *boldness* and *self-confidence*. That's why we fall into their trap—even if it means religious grandstanding.

But Jesus was so convinced of the power of love that He said, "If someone strikes you on the right cheek, turn to him the other also. And if someone wants to sue you and take your tunic, let him have your cloak as well. If someone forces you to go one mile, go with him two miles" (Matthew 5:39–41). *Be powerless.*

Paul was so convinced of the power of love that he said, "Do not be overcome by evil, but overcome evil with good" (Romans 12:21).

Love conquers all.

It comes down to this in the end: Jesus *possessed* power—He was not possessed *by* it. He set the pace for us as men by becoming a servant. That kind of power, that kind of love, opens hearts. It reveals Christ. It affirms and strengthens other people.

In the Father's eyes, it changes a willful man into a willing son of God.

SOUL OPENER

Do You Have a Problem With Power?

Take the following short quiz. Check the reactions that best describe you. Or, if you're up for a real challenge, invite your wife to check the answers for you!

When in disagreement with your wife, which is usually more important to you?

☐ a. Being right
☐ b. Really hearing her out

When you have been too harsh with your child, what do you do?

☐ a. Firmly plant your feet and tell yourself, *It's his/her fault. He/she drove me to it.*
☐ b. Ask your child's forgiveness.

When you lose a game in sports, what's your attitude?

☐ a. "The other guy has one up on me. I'll have to get him back."
☐ b. "I accept the loss. I don't regret having played the game."

On the job, when somebody challenges your thinking on a project, how do you feel?

☐ a. Threatened or frustrated that they'll get in my way or slow down my agenda.
☐ b. Enlivened and challenged to consider their perspective.

When motivating people to accomplish tasks (employees, your kids, others), what approach do you most often use?

☐ a. "Do this, or I'll make things difficult for you."
☐ b. "Do this because it will help you to succeed."

In a group setting, when someone captures all the attention with a joke or interesting story, what is your reaction?

☐ a. I tense up and resent the fact that they're "stealing the show," or I wait impatiently for the chance to jump in with my next story.
☐ b. I enjoy hearing someone else express himself.

If you checked "a" on one or more of these questions, you may have a problem with power. Recognizing this is the first step toward discovering that you have to release some control in order to walk with Jesus. Take some time to prayerfully reflect on which is greater in you—the power of love or the love of power.

Here is a sample prayer:

> Lord, when I am wrong, make me willing to change. When I am right, make me easy to live with. So strengthen me that the power of my example will far exceed the authority of my rank.[3]

Notes

1. As quoted in *Along the Road to Manhood*, Stu Weber (Sisters, OR: Multnomah Press, 1995), p. 21.
2. Anthony Campolo, Jr., *The Power Delusion* (Wheaton, IL: Victor Books, 1983), p.11.
3. Pauline H. Peters

Part Three

A Sharing Soul
(The Man God *Fuses*)

CHAPTER EIGHT

As for Me and My House

"The Lord's curse is on the house of the wicked, but he blesses the home of the righteous."

Proverbs 3:33

"Susan came into the bathroom while I was getting dressed, and she says I was singing, which so confused her that she cried, 'Mom, did we win?' and I said, 'No, you kids got a father back, and I got my husband back' "

—Betty Ford, 1976
(the morning after her husband lost the presidential election).

"A leader is a person with a magnet in his heart and a compass in his head."

—Robert Townsend

The first organization God ever called a man to lead was a family.

Before there were corporations to run, buildings to be built, budgets to prepare, paychecks to pick up, bank accounts to monitor, sporting events to attend, even church committees to run (or a church *at all*), God created man. And then God presented that man with a family.

When God created man and breathed within him a soul, resident in that soul was all the potential to lead, nourish, and provide for his wife and children. The picture is clear. As God was faithful in tending to His creation, so He would enable man to be faithful in caring for his wife and children. The plan was masterful.

Ironically, man took a detour that led him away from God's path.

Our first parents' sin against God darkened and confused humanity's collective soul. Not only was Adam's standing with God affected, his abilities to *husband*, to *father*, and to *lead* were severely impaired. This impairment became our spiritual heritage. The Bible characterizes this intrinsic flaw in us plainly: "There is a way that seems right to a man, but in the end it leads to death" (Proverbs 14:12).

When man took his life into his own hands, the consequences went deep: the spiritual and moral compass within every one of us has been smashed. Without a connection to God a man is lost—when he thinks a direction is north, it may not be north at all.

For this reason we have a world full of men who are trying to lead their families with a broken compass. We have put ourselves in the driver's seat, and the effects are devastating.

As a result of Adam's sin, man's everyday life is infected with what the Bible calls a curse. God gave the bad news to Adam this way: "Cursed is the ground because of you; through painful toil you will eat of it all the days of your life. It will produce thorns and thistles for you, and you will eat the plants of the field. By the sweat of your brow you will eat your food until you return to the ground, since from it you were taken; for dust you are and to dust you will return" (Genesis 3:17–19).

The curse was not work itself, but new difficulties would characterize a man's work. His ability to keep his relationships to family and to work in proper order were affected.

To put it plainly, as a result of sin man has a built-in tendency to look for himself, lose himself, or hide himself within his work. Work becomes his preoccupation—he is consumed with it and often over-committed to it. This tendency in men has left many wives and children sorely lacking in intimacy and support.

A man's performance rating at work may soar. Or he may become preoccupied with a career that's run aground. But when his relationships at home sink under the weight of his work preoccupations, he has lost his soul-connection to life itself and a higher purpose for living.

Finding Our Way Back

Many men want to discover how to care for their wives and children, but often don't know where to begin. Frequently, men move around their families, that is, live in the same house but fail to consistently engage their wife and children in meaningful relationships. At worst, some men have become dead-beat dads who have traded a real family for a fleeting, shallow, sex-based relationship; or, they become abusers of their wife and children.

Most common are the guys who have become disinterested or dis-engaged from their families. I have seen a lot of Christian men who fall into this category, wondering how to make a change. There are even some men who would swear they are the spiritual leader in their home—when they are as out of touch with the needs of their family as they can be.

Read the following section with an open mind.

Engaging the Disengaged Dad

The disinterested or disengaged dad is vividly described in this true story by a woman who had one:

> One morning, my father didn't get up and go to work. He went to the hospital and died the next day. I hadn't thought that much about him before. He was just someone who left and came home and seemed glad to see everyone. He opened the jar of pickles when no one else could. He was the only one in the house who wasn't afraid to go into the basement by himself. Whenever I played house, the mother doll had a lot to do. I never knew what to do with the daddy doll, so I had him say, "I'm going off to work now." And I put him under the bed. The funeral was in our living room, and a lot of people came and brought all kinds of good food and cakes. We never had so much company before. I went to my room and felt under the bed for the daddy doll, and when I found him, I dusted him off and put him on my bed. He never did any-thing. I didn't know his leaving would hurt so much.[1]

For some women and children, there is a man at home most every night, but he doesn't seem to be with them at all. He may be too com-mitted to his family to ever leave them, but he is reluctant or unable to genuinely open up his life and heart to them. Ironically, he can spend incredible amounts of energy providing the things they perhaps need the least. He may be an expert at fulfilling the family's financial com-mitments and not even be in the starting blocks when it comes to build-ing or replenishing their souls.

Does any of this sound familiar? Do you feel disengaged or even a bit frustrated about fulfilling your role as husband or father? Perhaps you find yourself asking some of the same questions I've asked myself about it all: *Where is the book on how to head up a home? What does it take to succeed at being a father? a husband? Can I be what they need and still be myself? What will it require of me? How can I tell if I'm doing it right or wrong? Who will let me know?*

Dean Merrill is one dad who definitely felt this way. His words strike a chord within:

> If you're a carpenter, you haven't forgotten your five long years of apprenticeship.
>
> If you're an attorney, you'll always remember the rigors of law school.
>
> If you're a salesman, you recall the break-in period and are still taking time for periodic seminars and training sessions on sales techniques.
>
> If you're a minister, hardly a week goes by without your talking about seminary days.
>
> Some of us have spent four, five, six, or even seven long years in colleges and graduate schools getting ready to make a living. Others of us have learned on the job as we've watched, questioned, and imitated a master craftsman of our trade.
>
> Men have another job that carries a good deal of responsibility and a lot of challenge. We can succeed at it or fail so badly that we lose the job and all it means to us. It's called husbanding. Being the head of our house. Who trained us for this job?
>
> Most of us have to answer no one—and that's a tragedy. It's not our fault. It's just the way things have worked out. We've been so busy learning how to read profit margin reports and rebuild carburetors that we haven't had time to study husbanding. And even if we'd asked, there was no one to teach us.[2]

Leading a family requires much from a man. Contrary to some notions, it does not "come naturally." The fall of man saw to that. I am convinced, however, that the potential to become an effective husband and father is still present within every man. But it must be cultivated or drawn out by connecting ourselves to God through prayer, the Word of God, and by opening up to other godly men who can provide examples of what an effective husband and father looks like.

This ancient Chinese proverb paints a vivid picture:

> If there is light in the soul,
> There will be beauty in the person.
> If there is beauty in the person,
> There will be harmony in the house.

If there is harmony in the house,
There will be order in the nation.
If there is order in the nation,
There will be peace in the world.

Man With a Mission

When it comes to examples, Joshua stands out among the husbands and fathers of Scripture. His unflinching commitment to his family and to his country paints a compelling picture of what goes into building a home where God is honored. Joshua endured wars and many other hardships—yet he held to his faith and his commitment to God right to his death bed. What was it within this man that gave him the strength and resolve to face the challenges that surrounded him?

The final statement of the man who was summoned by the Spirit to fill Moses' shoes is classic: "But as for me and my household . . . we will serve the Lord" (Joshua 24:15). Many Christian men typically focus on Joshua the hero—the man called to lead the nation of Israel into the enemy-infested Promised Land. But do we recognize Joshua the family man—the one who first and foremost led his family flock in the direction of God's will?

Foundations on Which to Build a Home

What intrigues me the most about Joshua as a family man is his vision and conviction. Not only did he have a clear understanding of where and how he needed to lead his family, he had the strength of soul to do it. Such soul-strength, I believe, came to Joshua through the conflicts and challenges he endured, while at the same time he surrendered to God for the *wisdom* to know how to handle the obstacles before him.

Wrapped up in his great proclamation are four solid foundation stones on which a man can stabilize his own soul—and build his family as well.

First, Joshua made a commitment to God.

Before Joshua could speak for his wife and children, he had to speak for himself and his own relationship to God. For a man to lead his family in following Jesus collectively, he must first make the decision to follow Christ himself. Joshua could confidently say, "As for me . . ." because he'd made a solid choice to grow in his own relationship with God. We learn that even as a young aide to Moses, Joshua would linger at prayer long after Moses had returned to camp (see Exodus 33:11). The determination to lead a family in God's way can only be sustained when it flows from a man's own spirit-to-Spirit connection with God. The man who authentically loves and knows God will want his wife and children to know the same.

Second, Joshua had vision for his family.

As a child you were no doubt asked the question, "What do you want to be when you grow up?" Now that you're an adult, maybe the questions have changed to "What do you want to do when you retire?" or "Where would you like to travel?" But has anyone ever asked you, "What do you want your *children* to be like when they grow up? What kind of people do you hope they will be? What kind of faith do you hope they will have?"

Joshua's sense of responsibility obviously went well beyond the management of his own personal schedule, finances, and behavior. He had a vision that included his wife and children.

Often today, in the name of entrepreneurship, men are incited to chase after visions that leave out their most priceless investments— their wife and children. Even in our church fellowships, often the man who is considered successful is the one who has the biggest house, the most expensive car, the largest bank account, the most impressive title.

Even magazine titles reveal much about our priorities—*Fortune, Money, Self, Success.*

Running against the grain of culture, the only thing God is impressed with is the greatness of a man's soul. Joshua seemed to know this. He was responsible for all of Israel, but his own family was not forgotten or dragged along behind. They had a home in his soul. What touched them also touched him.

Third, Joshua took his motivation from God's purposes. And he set his will firmly in that direction.

Let me approach this by asking a question: When did we, as men, stop leading our families in doing what *is right* and begin letting them get away with doing whatever *feels right*?

The answer is probably when we started allowing *ourselves* to do whatever feels right, instead of learning from God how to obey and do what is right.

As men, it's time to reset our moral and spiritual foundations; time to lead from a deep-soul connection to God's standards and not from our own what-feels-right standards.

In saying this, I am *not* advocating tyrannical male dominance. I do, however, believe that men must become effective as leaders. And our moral and spiritual guidance is needed as never before.

There is a time when a man must draw the line and say to his child, "You are not going to that party because I am not comfortable with the fact that no chaperones will be present." There is a time when a man must say to his family, "We are turning the television off and returning the video to the store. I will not allow this kind of language or these kinds of images to fill our home." There is a time when a man must take an active role in directing the souls of his wife and children, rather than settling back into a role that is compromisingly reactive.

Chuck Swindoll urges:

> It is absolutely imperative, men, that we fight our tendency to be passive in matters pertaining to the home. The passive husband continues to be one of the most common complaints I hear from troubled homes. Men, *get with it*! Your wife will grow in her respect for you as soon as she sees your desire to take the leadership and management of the home.[3]

And a Promise Keepers leader asserts:

> I can hear you saying, "I want to be a [leader in my home]. Where do I start?"
>
> The first thing you do is sit down with your wife and say something like this: "Honey, I've made a terrible mistake. I've given you my role. I gave up leading the family, and I forced you to take my place. Now I must reclaim that role."
>
> Don't misunderstand what I'm saying here. I'm not suggesting that you ask for your role back, I'm urging you to *take it back*. If you simply ask for it, your wife is likely to say, "Look, for the last ten years, I've had to raise these kids, look after the house, and pay the bills. I've had to get a job and still keep up my duties in the home. I've had to do my job *and* yours. You think I'm going to just turn everything back over to you?"
>
> Your wife's concerns may be justified. Unfortunately, however, there can be no compromise here. If you're going to lead, you must lead. Be sensitive. Listen. Treat the lady gently and lovingly. But *lead*![4]

Joshua said, "We will serve the Lord." He was active in his spiritual leadership. With a made-up mind, he had a vision of what his family should be. He did not hesitate to assert his influence and his energy toward that end. He *led* his family.

Every man is called by God and the truth of Scripture to be active and engaged in spiritual leadership at home. *We motivate by example.*

You and I need every ounce of influence and energy we can find to lead our families closer to God. After all, we have been appointed to lead our children from their desert experience of adolescence into the promised land of adulthood; no one else has been appointed by God to do that.

Fourth, Joshua's goal and mission were clear—to "serve the Lord."

Loving, honoring, serving God—these were the focal points of Joshua's life. It focused who he was as a man, a military leader, a husband, and a father. Can it be any clearer to us what passion fueled this man's life? His soul was fixed on the goal of serving the purposes of God. Whether he was on the battlefield or correcting his children, Joshua was centered on God.

Jerry White says, "Ordinary people accomplish extraordinary things by focusing their lives." Joshua was a focused man determined, by God's grace, to lead his flock . . . his family.

SOUL OPENER

Drawing Closer to Your Family

"Awake, my soul!"

Psalm 57:8

While at my place of work, many things require my focused attention. It is easy to forget the needs of my family. I can even hide from those needs while at work.

As I head home, it helps to reorient myself and consciously lay aside my work focus. I do this by actively refocusing my thoughts on family plans, needs, and goals. Because so much is asked of us as husbands and fathers, we need to get mentally, spiritually, and motivationally ready to return home a good while before we enter the door.

One of the ways I do this is by asking myself some questions:

- *I wonder how Pam's day went?*
- *I wonder what the kids faced at school today?*
- *How can I best reconnect with them within the first few minutes of walking in the door?*
- *What can we do together tonight?*
- *What affirmations can I express to Pam and the kids to remind them how special they are to me?*

- *If someone had a bad day, how can I lift the load?*
- *If someone has failed or made a serious mistake, what instruction, correction, or guidance can I give?*

These questions work wonders when it comes to getting me in a home mode. I find that when I prepare myself, I am more open, more relaxed, and more upbeat when I step through the door.

Notes

1. Taken from *Tender Warrior*, Stu Weber (Sisters, OR: Multnomah Books, 1993), p. 28.
2. From the booklet, "The Loving Leader: A Man's Role at Home," Dean Merrill, Focus on the Family, 1993, pp. 3–4.
3. Charles R. Swindoll, *Strike the Original Match* (Sisters, OR: Multnomah Press, 1980), p. 51.
4. *Seven Promises of a Promise Keeper*, various authors (Colorado Springs, CO: Focus on the Family Publishing, 1994), pp. 79–80.

CHAPTER NINE

Naked . . . and Unashamed

"The man [Adam] and his wife were both naked, and they felt no shame."

Genesis 2:25

"The one thing most men lack is the one thing most women want: intimacy."[1]

—Patrick Morley

Nakedness is compelling.

In Eden, we are told, Adam and Eve were "naked [and] they were not ashamed." The environment must have been heaven on earth. A man. A woman. A garden full of beauty and nourishment. God watching over them. Protected. Safe. Free . . . no clothing necessary.

To Adam and Eve it wasn't nakedness—as we know it—it was normalcy. Their sinless environment and natures permitted them to share in absolute openness. After all, they had nothing to hide. They were altogether free, in the truest sense, to be themselves completely and without apology. No hang ups, no inhibitions, no fear.

When Adam first gazed upon the magnetic beauty of Eve, his exclamation said it all: "This is now bone of my bones and flesh of my flesh; she shall be called 'woman,' for she was taken out of man" (Genesis 2:23). In other words, "You are a part of me and I am a part of you. We exist to be united, to share deeply—to be *one*."

The passage continues: "For this reason a man will leave his father and mother and be united to his wife, and they will become one flesh. The man and his wife were both naked, and they felt no shame" (Genesis 2:24–25).

One fascinated husband writes:

> I sometimes wonder what it is like for nudists: whether they ever really get used to it. As for me, I still haven't gotten used to seeing my own wife naked. It's almost as if her body is shining with a light, too bright to look at for very long. I cannot take my eyes off her—and yet I must. To gaze too long or too curiously is, even with her, a breach of propriety, almost a crime. It is not like watching a flower or creeping up to spy on an animal in the wild. No, my wife's body is brighter and more fascinating than a flower, shier than any animal, and more breathtaking than a thousand sunsets. To me her body is the most awesome thing in creation. Trying to look at her, just trying to take in her wild, glorious beauty, so free and primal, so utterly unchanged since the beginning of time (despite what evolutionists may think), I catch a small glimpse of what it means that men and women have been made in the image of God. If even the image is this dazzling, what must the Original be like?
>
> In marriage we learn that nakedness, like God Himself, is inexhaustibly contemplatible. We can never really "see" it, never quite look directly at it, for at one and the same time it is both a revelation and a darkness, a shining and a secret. That shy but driving curiosity we have about other human bodies will be with us all our lives. There is a peeping Tom in all of us, for we can never see enough, never drink our fill. The truth is this is grossly mirrored in the man who is a slave of lust, for whom one stripper or one glossy photograph is never enough. But such lust of the eyes and of the flesh is only the perversion of a perfectly natural and healthy curiosity, healthy because it is the Lord Himself Who made us curious, Who has caused us to be fascinated with one another's flesh. It is God Who has given the naked body its shining glory and Who has done so for the sole purpose of making it a marvelous harbinger of His Own infinitely more lustrous glory.[2]

Naked and unashamed. Perhaps these two adjectives describe best the intimacy that a man and wife share within the "marriage bed" (Hebrews 13:4), which Scripture describes as honorable and pure. The New Testament paints a picture of this place as being the closest thing to Eden a man may know in this life. A man and a woman—enveloped in one another—open, uninhibited, abandoned, unburdened.

And this state of open bliss was God's idea.

Intimacy Threatened

Then sin entered Eden. Instead of living to serve God and one another, Adam and Eve suddenly became all too aware of themselves. Enter selfishness.

The first change was that Adam and Eve became painfully aware of their vulnerability and shame. "Then the eyes of both of them were opened, and they realized they were naked" (Genesis 3:7). R. C. Sproul notes that it is interesting what Scripture does *not* say: "Their eyes were opened and they became aware of their *guilt*," or "they became aware of their *sin*," or "they became aware of the *crime* they had committed." Rather, they were aware of their nakedness.

From that moment on, it has been cover-up city.

All at once they "heard the sound of the Lord God as he was walking in the garden in the cool of the day, and they hid from the Lord God among the trees" (Genesis 3:8). Ironic, isn't it? God's created children trying to hide from their Creator under the cover of His creation.

And then God asked that eternally haunting question:

"Where are you?" (v. 9).

And Adam's response reveals the struggle of his anguished soul: "I heard you in the garden, and I was afraid because I was naked; so I hid" (v. 10).

"Who told you that you were naked?" God responded, searching the soul of man more deeply. "Have you eaten from the tree that I commanded you not to eat from?" (v. 11).

While Adam is riveted on the results of the tragedy ("I am afraid" and "I am exposed"), God probes to reveal the source of the dilemma: "Did you do what I instructed you not to do?" God speaks the truth, and man runs from it. How many times has that happened since that dreadful day? In what ways are we hiding from God's revealing words at this very moment? What peaceful freedom with God, and our lives, have we sacrificed along the way?

In that tragic moment, the man and woman lost their sense of *couple-identity*. Instead of seeing Eve as bone of his bone, she became the estranged "other." Someone to accuse. Rather than sharing, they withdrew. In that moment, man not only lost his right standing with God, he lost a right relationship with his wife.

And so a chasm opened. And the gulf has grown ever since.

To this day, nakedness is compelling. A man has a deep inner longing to look upon and to hold his wife unclothed, uninhibited, and know that she is utterly abandoned to him. And in a unique way a woman also has a craving to look upon and to touch her husband's soul, uncovered, uninhibited, and to know that he is utterly abandoned and open to her.

A naked body.

A naked soul.

I do not mean by this to imply that a man does not desire to be close to his wife spiritually or a wife to her husband physically. But for some reason, men seek out counseling most often because of sexual frustration, while women seek counsel most often because of relational frustrations.

Virtual Intimacy

We live in an age of fast food, dual incomes, and entertainment saturation. We put far more into entertainment and amusement than we do into marriage and family. Technology is pulling us into the faces of computer terminals and away from those of our spouse and kids. We thought technology was supposed to help us get more done in less time and free us up to be at home more, but we forgot to factor in something—selfishness and greed. Instead of more time for the people in our lives, we have become even more compulsive, determined to build, achieve, and attain—while our marriage and our kids are neglected.

Intimacy is something we know very little about today. Too often we are unwilling to invest what intimacy requires—ourselves, our devotion, our attention, our time. Thus, we live in a world that wants "intimacy on call"—a cheap imitation. We have gone through the sexual revolution, and human nakedness is now big business. Instead of being preserved for the place God intended—the sacred "marriage bed"—it has been broadcast into homes and projected on the silver screen. Still, our culture is preoccupied with nakedness.

Sproul has said, "We are looking for a place where we can be naked and unashamed."[3] We all carry a longing to get back to the Garden of sweet freedoms within the context of a meaningful relationship.

"God created this one-flesh experience to be the most intense height of physical intimacy and the most profound depth of spiritual oneness between husband and wife."[4]

Starving for It

Many wives and husbands today are starving for more intimacy in their lives, and especially in their marriage. But intimacy only comes when sufficient trust and openness occur within a relationship. Then an individual can express his needs, hurts, dreams, and desires, feeling safe and confident. When an atmosphere full of acceptance grows, allowing that kind of expression, it does more than warm a marriage. Something greater occurs. Two lives have a chance to unite and blend. Souls connect.

Consider this telling letter, received by a pastor from a lonely lady:

> The kids are in bed. There's nothing on TV tonight. I ask my husband if he minds if I turn the tube off. He grunts.
>
> As I walk to the set my mind is racing. Maybe, just maybe, tonight we'll talk. I mean, we'll have a conversation that consists of more than my usual question with his mumbled one-word answer or, more accurately, no answer at all.
>
> Silence—I live in a world with continuous noise but, between him and myself, silence. Please—oh God, let him open up. I initiate (once again; for the thousandth time). My heart pounds—oh how can I word it this time? What can I say that will open the door to just talk? I don't have to have meaningful conversation. Just something!
>
> As I open my mouth—he gets up and goes to the bedroom. The door closes behind him. The light showing under the door gives way to darkness. So does my hope.
>
> I sit alone on the couch. My heart begins to ache. I'm tired of being alone. Hey, I'm married. I have been for years. Why do I sit alone?[5]

"Into-Me-See"

Rod Cooper describes intimacy as "into-me-see." I like that. It says much about what intimacy brings and calls for. Undoubtedly, the man who chooses to give his wife genuine intimacy gives her much more than a marriage license. He gives her himself—unmasked, uncovered, and unlimited.

Dinah Craik described intimacy vividly well over a century ago:

> Oh the comfort, the inexpressible comfort
> of feeling safe with another person.
> Having neither to weigh thoughts nor measure words,
> but pouring them all right out just as they are,
> chaff and grain together—
> Certain that a faithful hand
> will take and sift them, keep what is worth keeping
> and with a breath of kindness blow the rest away.[6]

Intimacy cannot be forced or demanded. No remote control exists which, upon command, can summon the thoughts, concerns, feelings and longings of a spouse's soul to suddenly appear. Intimacy is something that must be drawn out in a relationship. Proverbs 20:5 says: "The purposes of a man's heart are deep waters, but a man of understanding draws them out."

Intimacy comes from the Latin *intimus*, meaning "inmost."

Approaching the "Holy of Holies"

The Old Testament paints a vivid picture of intimacy for us in the image of the tabernacle, the ancient Jews' center for worship. When God gave Moses directions for building the tabernacle, it included three main areas: first, the "outer court"; second, "the inner court"; and third, "the holiest of all," or the "holy of holies." These areas represented stages through which a worshiper would pass as he drew closer to God.

The "outer court" was where the public mingled and talked. The "inner court" was where the worshiper would meet a priest, confess sins, and offer a suitable sacrifice. The "holiest of all" was the place where the glory of God dwelt. His presence was there. You could not get any closer to the heart of God than in this sacred room. And yet it was such a holy place that an unauthorized individual who rushed into it would be struck dead. Careful preparation had to be made by the high priest to enter that holy place, and even he could only enter it once a year.

The human body, then, possesses a glory that is unique in all the earth (glory in the ordinary sense of "awe-inspiring beauty," but also in the special biblical sense of "the spirtual made visible"), and it is in the peculiar dazzle of nakedness that this glory is most obvious, most tantalizng and revealing. In human nakedness something is uncovered and shown to our eyes and to our souls which cannot be seen anywhere else, nor even begin to be imitated. The curtain of the holy of holies is pulled aside, and something crouches there in the half light, something utterly familiar yet stranger than a dream. Human beings are, after all, the only creatures which can be naked, the only creatures in which this bizarre unveiling can take place. For in everything else, whether animate or inanimate, nakedness is axiomatic. Trees may be clothed in their autumn splendor or the sea wear a mantle of light—but only by analogy with human clothing. Man alone puts an artificial covering over his body. Everything else stand stark, staring naked in the sight of God and is not ashamed.[7]

What does this say to us?

I believe these images help paint a picture of the couple that desires to grow closer to each other. Let's say, in a relational sense, that the "holiest of all" represents the soul of your spouse, the fountain of her emotions, hopes, dreams, hurts, and her faith. A husband or wife seeking to grow closer and more intimate with their spouse does so by carefully, respectfully entering that inmost place. As with the tabernacle, the soul of your spouse is a privileged place, reserved for the right person who will approach in an appropriate and sensitive manner.

Walter Wangerin, Jr., describes the sacred place of marital intimacy:

> Trust allows him, encourages her, to be naked before you and not ashamed. Naked physically: no part of the body is hidden since no curve of it will be hurt or troubled by embarrassment. Naked emotionally and spiritually: no part of the personality, no feeling, no memory or fear or internal delight need be hidden either, since *nothing* of your spouse will *be* hurt or abused or embarrassed.
>
> Trust allows him, encourages her, to present a whole self before you. And honesty in you, likewise, hides nothing of your whole self from your spouse."[8]

God never intended that we indiscriminately bear our souls to just anyone. No, God has designed us to be knit soul-to-soul with one other person in the deepest kind of honest intimacy.

Unclothed and Unashamed

Living life from the soul affects not only the way a man worships God, it impacts the way he makes love to his covenant bride. The fruit of the Spirit is not only promised to make him a better witness, but also a better lover.

What moment in a man's life can compare with that of the wedding night, when a beautiful woman takes off all her clothes and lies next to him in bed, and that woman is his wife? What can equal the surprise of finding out that the one thing above all others which mankind has been most enterprising and proficient in dragging through the dirt turns out in fact to be the most innocent thing in the world? Is there any other activity at all which an adult man and woman may engage in together (apart from worship) that is actually more childlike, more clean and pure, more natural and wholesome and unequivocally right than is the act of making love? For if worship is the deepest available form of communion with God, than surely sex is the deepest communion that is possible between human beings, and as such is something absolutely essential (in more than a biological way) to our survival. . . .

Marriage attacks orignal sin, in effect, at its visible root, in the shame of nakedness, and defeats and heals this shame by directly confronting it on the safe and holy ground of a covenant relationship. For a husband and wife to be naked together is like a kind of radiation treatment, the healing rays of which can be felt at the center of the soul. It is, as nearly as possible, a return to the very last statement the book of Genesis makes about mankind's state of innocence in Paradise: "The man and his wife were both naked, and they felt no shame" (Genesis 2:25).[9]

There are two places God has provided for us to be "naked" and "unashamed." Two places we can go.

The first place I can go and bear my soul without hesitation or reservation is into the presence of God. When I pray, I can tell Him everything, unload everything, because He knows me better than anyone else.

David was comfortable standing soul-bare and open in the presence of God. Consider his words:

> O Lord, you have searched me and you know me. You know when I sit and when I rise; you perceive my thoughts from afar . . . you are familiar with all my ways. . . . Where can I go from your Spirit? Where can I flee from your presence? If I go up to the heavens, you are there; if I make my bed in the depths, you are there. If I rise on the wings of the dawn, if I settle on the far side of the sea, even there your hand will guide me, your right hand will hold me fast" (Psalm 139:1–3, 7–10).

The writer of Hebrews painted a vivid picture of how a man stands before the presence and Word of God:

> For the word of God is living and active. Sharper than any double-edged sword, it penetrates even to dividing soul and spirit, joints and marrow; it judges the thoughts and attitudes of the heart. Nothing in all creation is hidden from God's sight. Everything is uncovered and laid bare before the eyes of Him to whom we must give account (Hebrews 4:12–13).

The second place I can go to be naked and unashamed is my marriage relationship. There is no place where I can be myself more freely and completely than when I am at home. At home, I don't have to act, perform, pretend, or strive. Why? Because, as an old song says, "The one who knows me best, loves me most."

No one knows me as well as my wife. My strengths, struggles, values, doubts, sins, accomplishments, fears, failures, and dreams. She knows all about me. I have become exposed to her and she to me. The veil has been removed—and it continues to be, more and more. And, amazingly, she still loves me—as I never dreamed I could be loved.

SOUL OPENER

Questions About Intimacy to Discuss
With Your Spouse

How close are you to your spouse? How comfortable are you unclothed—physically, and spiritually? Here are some questions you can use to carefully approach these sensitive and yet significant areas of your marriage partnership:

1. How did you feel after our wedding when we were en route to our room for the night? What was going through your mind and heart as you anticipated the consummation of our marriage? Be honest.
2. What was it like for you the first time you saw me naked? How did you feel when you first disrobed in front of me?
3. In what way is nakedness an important part of closeness in our marriage? How would it be different if it was not a part of our relationship?
4. Have I been as quick to expose my soul to you as I have my body? How can you tell?
5. When have our souls felt the closest as a couple?
6. Describe a time when you felt I really opened my soul to you? How did it affect our relationship? How did my doing that make you feel?
7. What is sexual intimacy like for you when our souls are distant?
8. What is sexual intimacy like for you when our souls are close? Is there a connection between spiritual intimacy and sexual intimacy in our relationship? Explain.
9. What could I do to make you more comfortable being physically close to me?
10. What could I do to make you more comfortable being spiritually close to me? Opening your heart to me more fully? Letting me into your life?

Notes

1. Patrick M. Morley, *Two-Part Harmony* (Nashville, TN: Thomas Nelson, 1994), p. 78.
2. Mike Mason, *The Mystery of Marriage* (Sisters, OR: Multnomah Press, 1985), pp. 113–114.
3. R.C. Sproul, Christian Marriage audio series (Ligonier Ministries).
4. Herbert J. Miles, *Sexul Happiness in Marriage* (Grand Rapids, MI: Zondervan Publishing, 1967), p. 28.
5. As quoted in "Now We're Talking! Questions to Build Intimacy with Your Spouse" (Focus on the Family, Colorado Springs, CO, 1996), pp.5–6.
6. As quoted in *Tender Warrior* by Stu Weber (Sisters, OR: Multnomah Press, 1993), p. 112.
7. Mason, pp. 115–116.
8. Walter Wangerin, Jr., *As for Me and My House: Crafting Your Marriage to Last* (Nashville, TN: Thomas Nelson Publishers, 1987), p. 189.
9. Mason, pp. 120–121.

CHAPTER TEN

Strengthening Your Soul Mate

*"There are three things that are too amazing for me, four that I do
not understand: the way of an eagle in the sky, the way of a snake on
a rock, the way of a ship on the high seas,
and the way of a man with a maiden."*

Proverbs 30:18–19

*"Let the wife make the husband glad to come home, and let him make
her sorry to see him leave."*

—Martin Luther

*"The most important thing a father can do for his children
is to love their mother."*

—Theodore Hesburgh, former president of Notre Dame

The note taped to the front door looked like an ordinary "reminder"
from Pam. Eager to head off to work while she was still sleeping, I
slipped the note in my appointment book and set off to meet my day.
I'd check the note later. Right now a schedule chock-full of "responsibilities" lay ahead.

Somewhere around lunchtime, I noticed the note again. It had
dropped out of my appointment book and lay on my desk still un-
touched. The first sentence seized something inside me.

It went something like this:

Robert,
  I don't know what's happened to us. The life we're now
living, from my view, is no life at all. At least, this is not what

I ever thought life would become. It feels like you're more married to your work than you are to me. I'm confused. And I don't know what to do with all that it's causing me to feel. Something is gone from our relationship.

There are times I almost wish your preoccupation was with another woman. Then I could tell her to "bug off!" This may come as a surprise to you, but something within me is dying. Something in our relationship is dying, and I don't know what to do about it.

I've tried in lots of little ways to talk with you about this, but you just aren't hearing me. Sure, you may listen. But I don't think you're really hearing me.

It's clear to me that you love what you do. Obviously. Because you give your best to it. Then there's little left for us. Our house isn't really a home to you. It's a hotel. You sleep and eat here. That's about it.

You're so creative at your work—I wish you would pour some of your creative energy into our home, into our children, into me.

Now we have a new baby in our lives, and she needs more than I can give her by myself. She needs a dad and I need a husband. Robert, I don't know where to turn next or what to do. You're not hearing me, so I don't know who to turn to. I have prayed about all of this, and I still find myself very frustrated.

Pam

For the first time in months, Pam's words penetrated the force fields surrounding me. I saw myself as a man busy living out his own interests. And I felt alarmed by the desperate tone of Pam's note.

She had expressed frustrations before. But I'd always viewed them as something we would work through. This was different, maybe because I now connected the words in this note with the look I'd been seeing on her face. The look I'd been ignoring . . . *hopelessness* . . . pain.

And I was overwhelmed with embarrassment. While helping other people, I'd totally overlooked my wife and family. What was I doing? How had I missed it? After all, I was *the pastor.* Two hundred teenagers and a couple dozen volunteer youth workers came to me for counsel and advice. Couples came to me for premarital and marriage counseling, and my files were full of prescriptions for enriching your marriage relationship!

When does the heart go out of a marriage? What restores it?

I could have argued and defended myself. *After all, I have so many demands on me. Pam knew I was going into ministry when she married me.* I could have rationalized, *It's only for a few years.* Or I could have attacked: *What about you? Remember when you . . . It drives me nuts when you . . .* None of these "lines" would restore anything. I knew. I'd watched dozens of other husbands use them on their wives, right in the very office where I was sitting.

I decided it was time to "wise up." So I read the note again, painful as it was, in order to let the full meaning of it go deep.

The note drove home one point loud and clear: *Our marriage had entered a danger zone.* The question tensing within my stomach now was, *What am I going to do about this?*

As I sat there thinking and praying, I remembered an old saying: *Desperate situations call for desperate actions.* By now, my busy agenda had paled in significance, and I made up my mind to do something I'd never done before.

I called a teenager from our youth group and asked if she'd baby-sit our toddler. Then I called Pam to let her know I'd read her note and really wanted some time with her.

To this day, I'm so thankful God gave me the good sense to open my day and my heart to Pam. For hours, in a quiet corner of our favorite restaurant, she poured out her soul. At first, I felt overwhelmed, because the note was a mere line drawing of the problem. What I heard painted her dilemma in living color. I tried to see myself through her eyes—and I came face-to-face with things that, quite honestly, I wanted to avoid. This was more than a case of a guy getting caught up in his work. I saw my selfishness. My preoccupations. My insensitivity.

I saw my failure. What scared me was the anger—the fury—that wanted to rise up and defend against the attacker.

Except the "attacker" was a soft-voiced, wounded soul, who had accepted my offer of a safe environment in which to speak!

In the next couple of hours, I saw what I'd done. I'd spent myself building a youth ministry, a team of youth workers, and my career. And I'd left unattended the thing which I'd contracted, before God, to build—my marriage and home. It seemed that while these other buildings were thriving, I'd hardly done more than put the frame up where Pam and our child were concerned. A sense of shame filled me. And then, just as important, an earnest desire to begin again, with God's help.

Souls at Odds

Pam and I both had much to learn about God's will for our marriage. And about ourselves. But we were eager to get to the source of our struggle and find solutions. As we dug into the Scriptures together, our search first took us all the way back to the Garden of Eden—and to some eye-opening discoveries from a familiar story.

In fact, most of us are so familiar with the story of the Fall, found in Genesis 3, that we may miss some of life's most important lessons.

Here's the first lesson we need to grasp—and it's a big one: *Sin came into the world through an invasion of selfishness in the soul of a man.* God's simple plan was ruined by disobedience on Adam's part, and the results were catastrophic. The image of God within Adam and Eve, within their souls, was shattered. In a moment's time he became preoccupied with self instead of being in awe of God and of His creation (v. 8). Where there had been love and trust, fear entered their relationship—both with God and with each other (v. 10). When God confronted Adam with his sin, Adam shamefully pointed to Eve—wanting to accuse and blame rather than protect her (v. 12). Now, instead of living at her side, he would live at odds with her—this woman whom God had created as his soul mate.

In the last chapter, we saw that one aspect of the curse was that man would suffer a preoccupation with his work to the neglect of his wife and children. This tendency would become one of the basic struggles and tensions in men—the struggle to make his mark, to achieve, to be respected and recognized as a person of skill and worth.

But there were also struggles and tensions for Eve as a result of the Fall. Increased pain in childbearing, for one. And, when it comes to marriage, a drive to find respect and recognition in the eyes of one man . . . who now, as it happens, wants to find his meaning and purpose *anywhere* but in relationships! God said, "Your desire will be for your husband" (3:16)—and He might as well have added, "Poor thing! Because his desire will be to build that business, get that promotion, bring home that bigger paycheck, and be able to buy more stuff, so he can feel good about himself!" Over the past several years, as Pam and I have continued to grow in this area, she has taught often on this subject. Her paraphrase of Genesis 3:16 goes something like this:

"As a result of the curse, a woman has a built-in tendency to look to her husband to meet many of her deepest needs. There can even be a tendency to expect him to be her all-in-all. To some women that might sound romantic. To others not. But it is definitely unrealistic. At its worst, it is borderline idolatrous. Although God has intended for man and woman to be true soul mates, there are many needs in a woman's soul that can only be met through a vital and personal relationship with God through the Lord Jesus. A woman needs the love, affection, encouragement, and support of her husband, but she cannot thrive without intimacy with God. This is the one relationship on which her soul must stand—founded in trust, growing in faith."

Talk about tension! In one corner stands the man who has a built-in soul tendency toward finding his sense of identity, significance, and security from his profession or career. He is poised to express his manhood and find his validation in the workplace. In the other corner stands the woman, who is soul-geared toward the man to whom she naturally looks for encouragement, tender care, romance, friendship, companionship, and affirmation.

The more Pam and I considered these passages and tendencies, the more we had to admit they are true in us, especially when we forgot that our one true source of life and well-being is *God alone.* Back when we first made these discoveries, I had to admit that after winning Pam's affection and entering into married life, I'd shifted my focus from pursuing her wholeheartedly to pursuing my goals at work. Pam, in turn, had to admit that though part of her feeling hurt was a result of my neglect, a bigger portion came from unrealistic and unbiblical expectations about our relationship.

It seemed to us then, as it does now, that growth as a couple—and as healthy, mature adults—would come only as we addressed these tendencies in our own souls. That is where we all have to begin.

The Soul of a Woman

One result of facing myself was a growing awareness of something I had virtually ignored: *the soul of my wife—her inner drives, desires, and needs—is shaped by the hand of God. As her husband, I have been called by God both to provide for her life needs and to nurture, cherish, cultivate, and care for her soul.* Clearly, the things my wife most vitally needs from me don't come from a title, a paycheck, big birthday gifts, or a kiss goodbye on the way out the door. Her needs are met when we face fears, challenges, stresses, confusion, temptations, and all of life's joys and sorrows . . . *together.*

This is what Paul had in mind when he instructed the men of the Ephesian church. Consider his charge:

> Husbands, *go all out in your love* for your wives, exactly as Christ did for the church—a love marked by *giving*, not getting. Christ's love makes the church whole. His *words evoke* her beauty. Everything he does and says is designed to *bring*

the best out of her, dressing her in dazzling white silk, radiant with holiness. And that is how husbands ought to love their wives. They're really doing themselves a favor—since they're already "one" in marriage.

No one abuses his own body, does he? No, he feeds and pampers it. That's how Christ treats us, the church, since we are part of his body. And this is why a man leaves father and mother and cherishes his wife. No longer two, they become "one flesh." This is a huge mystery, and I don't pretend to understand it all. What is clearest to me is the way Christ treats the church. And this provides a good picture of how each husband is to treat his wife, loving himself in loving her, and how each wife is to honor her husband (Ephesians 5:25–33, *The Message*, emphasis mine).

Paul makes clear the way in which God calls a man to invest himself in the life, heart, and soul of his wife. He must love her [cherish her] . . . give himself to her [as Christ gave himself for the Church] . . . cleanse her soul . . . present her radiant [vibrant, whole, alive within] . . . feed her . . . care for her . . . bond with her, soul to soul. Paul's passage is an invitation to me to know my wife more completely, and to be known by her.

You may be saying, "That's what I want to do. There is a part of me that wants that kind of relationship with my wife. I want her as my soul mate, but I don't know where or how to begin."

Richard Halverson, former chaplain to the U.S. Senate, after sixty-nine years of life and forty-two years of marriage, puts the ball in our court:

> It is my deep, settled conviction that one hundred percent of the responsibility for the sustenance of the marriage relationship belongs to the husband. The Scriptures tell us that as husbands we need to model ourselves after Jesus Christ, who gave himself up in every way in order to present His bride to himself without blemish or stain or spot or wrinkle.[1]

As a man and as head of my home, it is *my* responsibility to initiate God's purposes. Facing the wake-up call, I knew that I had some important steps to take to rebuild my marriage and to strengthen the soul of my wife.

For starters, I discovered that I had much to learn when it came to the soul of my spouse (and of women in general). The lenses through which I had been viewing her were shaded with the sinful tendencies resident in my own soul. Not really knowing Pam and the condition and needs of her inner life, I was expecting and demanding many unreasonable things from her out of my selfishness. Our souls were coexisting, while instead they needed to be united and blended.

Taking a closer look, I discovered seven things about a woman's soul that I wish I had been told years earlier.

Principle #1: The last thing you naturally feel like doing is probably the thing she needs the most.

Because men and women are "wired" so differently, many times (if not most) a man's natural inclinations toward her are not the most effective. In fact, they may be the least effective. Not at all unlike a missionary who enters a foreign culture, the wise man will study his wife, endeavor to discern her needs, and learn how to speak her language the best he can. Such a determined and sensitive approach will save him months, if not years, of anguish. And it will bring his wife great fulfillment. Every step a man takes out of his comfort zone to cultivate intimacy with his wife will come back to bless him.

Principle #2: What I'm quick to forget she's long to remember.

Generally speaking, women are more tuned-in to the emotional details of life than men. The "little things" not only *mean* the most to them, they are *felt* the most. The tender word before saying goodbye. The second kiss on the way out the door. The "I love you so much" tagged on to the end of a note or phone message. These are the soul-builders that men tend to see as insignificant and unnecessary. On the contrary, they are often the assurances that a woman's soul clings to throughout the day.

Principle #3: Don't criticize the words of her mouth; learn about the meditations of her heart.

Throughout the first few years of our marriage, my mind possessed an "attitude detector" that was often set on "hypersensitive"—especially when we had an argument. For example, whenever Pam would say something like, "You *never* come home on time," or "You *always* forget to pick up your dirty socks," the alarm would go off! My response went something like this: "Aha, I caught you. I *never*?? I *always*?? How can you possibly say that? There have been days when I have come home on time and times when I have picked up my socks!"

In my defensiveness, I missed the point. Pam's intention was not to write me off, but to wake me up to a real struggle she was having with me. My best tack would've been to study her heart instead of hair-splitting her word choices.[2]

Principle #4: My vulnerable abruptness needs the tempering effect of her feminine intuition about people.

It is uncanny to me how much more aware my wife is of the emotional needs of people than I am. I can chalk some of it off to her spiritual giftedness, but I'm convinced it is generally true of most women. At first, I resented her suggestions as to how I should reach out to the people in my life. By this juncture, I've come to view it as a great blessing, as a "balancer," because she's almost always on target. Now, instead of resenting the suggestions, I solicit them!

Principle #5: She is more intrigued (i.e., "turned-on") by character than by performance.

I used to think the primary things that would continue to attract my wife to me and make our marriage a great one were success on the job, a bigger paycheck, lots of fun trips, and sexual fulfillment. Boy, was I wrong. The longer I'm married the more clear it has become that those things are only the icing on the cake. The "cake" is consistency, character, promise-keeping, faithfulness, comfort, and encouragement.

Principle #6: The best way I can strengthen our marriage covenant is by being sensitive to and very encouraging of her relationship with God.

My wife's soul is never more strengthened or encouraged by me than when I speak of her relationship with God. When I ask her how her walk with Christ is going and when I share the insights flowing from my walk with Him, I build her up on the inside. Most women find such soul sensitivity absolutely irresistible. It is the thing that makes a Christian marriage truly *Christian.*

Principle #7: As sex is an expression (and "gauge") of our physical intimacy, so prayer together is or our spiritual intimacy.

I am convinced that part of the genius of God's plan in creating this thing called marriage was more than procreation. In the multiplied millions of marriages that will take place this year, there is the potential for something even more. Marriage is not just a parenting partnership; it is a prayer partnership. Through the uniting of couples committed to Christ, God establishes homes where children will be raised according to His ways and battle stations where prayers will be lifted up consistently to Him.

The wise man will pray often with his wife.

Soul Openers

Twenty Ways to Draw Closer to Your Soul Mate

1. Instead of making a business appointment for lunch, call your wife and tell her you want to meet and have lunch with her. Or let her know you're picking it up and will bring it home. Over lunch spend time getting up to speed on her "soul condition."

2. Take a few minutes to write some romantic one-liners on Post-It notes and place them in surprisingly strategic places throughout your home (i.e., inside her coat pocket, in a kitchen cabinet, on the bathroom mirror, etc.).

3. Give her a call in the middle of the day and tell her, "I'm just checking to see how your day is going."

4. When you see her overwhelmed with her life, ask her if she could use a hug. Give her a supportive one, and, while you're holding her, offer up a simple prayer to God on her behalf.

5. At the beginning of the week, before flying out the door, ask your wife, "Honey, what are some things I could do to help make your week a better one?" Be sure to follow through on what you commit to.

6. Plan a morning or afternoon hike together at some scenic area nearby. Make sure you set up the baby-sitting arrangements, if you really want to surprise her.

7. Grab your bikes and go for a short bike-ride together after supper.

8. Write a poem or a paragraph or two about what she means to you. It doesn't have to sound like Whittier or Longfellow to please her, as long as it's *you*. Print it out on a laser printer and frame it for her. Let the world know how you feel about her.

9. While you're out on a shopping expedition, get sidetracked on purpose and take your wife out to lunch or to coffee. Pick a place you know she'll like and focus your conversation and attention fully on her.

10. Pick up a journal for the two of you to chronicle the great times you have together. When you are on vacation or extended dates, keep a running record of where you went, what you did, where you ate, special memories, etc. As the years pass, you will find this to be a tremendous resource for reminiscing.

11. Keep a journal with your wife that includes a running chronicle of your children's lives. These don't have to be lengthy. Record major events, significant accomplishments, memorable words, spiritual growth, and character development observed. As your kids get older, this becomes a helpful tool to reflect on, reference, and read to your kids

as you watch them emerge into adults.

12. Go to the bookstore together, browse your favorite sections, and buy something new. Then, go out for coffee and discuss what you have discovered.

13. Get tickets for your favorite sports team and, instead of going with the guys, take your wife.

14. When you notice her general motivation waning, ask her to describe how she's doing emotionally in the words of a weather forecast (i.e., sunny, partly cloudy, thunderstorms, etc.)

15. Make it a point to "change gears" motivationally and intentionally on the way home from work. In order to re-gear and get into a family mode, pick a landmark that can serve to remind you en route to do this. Some great "gear-changing" questions to ask yourself and to enliven your sensitivities include: What challenges has my wife faced today? What is foremost on her mind? Has she had a chance to unload or unwind today? What are some of the things she most needs to discuss? What is the current condition of her "emotional bank"? What can I do to build her up in her soul?

16. Periodically plan a "passionate getaway" with your wife. Block out a few days on your calendar, making sure they are days she has clear, and plan a romantic weekend together. Many hotels offer affordable packages. Keep it a surprise as long as you can, and determine to initiate it yourself—pick the place, book the reservations, line up the baby-sitter, etc. One way to announce it to her is to give her a card and a gift of a new negligee.

17. Invite your wife to hold you accountable emotionally. If you request that she regularly ask you the hard questions, welcome them when she does so it won't seem to her or to you that she is nagging. The hard questions might include: How do you guard yourself morally? Are you ever tempted by or attracted to other women? How do sensual images in the media affect you as a man?

18. Invite your wife to give you a list of her top ten prayer needs. Commit to pray with her about them regularly and chronicle together the answers God brings.

19. Give her grace when she needs it the most. When she finishes the day with more "errors" than "runs," show her loving support. If she gets a dent in the car, discount the minor accident and be thankful she was not injured. Let her know you love her. Hugs do a much better repair job than reprimands.

20. Make a trip to a Christian bookstore and pick out a devotional

book or Bible study that you can complete together. Wrap it up with two coffee mugs and surprise her. Then put it to work!

Notes

1. Richard Halverson, *No Greater Power* (Sisters, OR: Multnomah, Press, 1986), p. 188.
2. Two books to help open a man's eyes to the needs of a woman that I highly recommend: *If He Only Knew* by Gary Smalley and *The Five Love Languages* by Dr. Gary Chapman.
3. A book that will encourage your prayer relationship with your spouse is *Praying With the One You Love* by Art Hunt (Multnomah Books, 1996).

CHAPTER ELEVEN

Father, Guide, and Helper

"You know that we dealt with each of you as a father deals with his own children, encouraging, comforting and urging you to live lives worthy of God, who calls you into his kingdom and glory."

1 Thessalonians 2:11–12

"You thought maybe God called himself 'Father' after you, to give you an illustration of what He's like? No way. He decided to call you 'father' after Him, to give you an illustration of what you're to be like as a father."[1]

—Anne Ortland

Jonathan Edwards, the great New England theologian and revivalist of the eighteenth century's Great Awakening, had deep convictions about a man's role in his home. "A home needs to be run like a little church," he said. And every father, as "pastor," is responsible not only for the physical needs of his wife and children but for watching over their souls, as well. In Edwards' mind, it was his ministry in the home that qualified him to minister in the church.

There is probably no role in all of life that's more intriguing, challenging, rewarding, and at times heartrending, than watching over the soul of a child. Unfortunately, as we urge children to "grow up" and assume responsibility, we often feed and encourage every part of their life except the spirit. We encourage them intellectually, so they can "get the grades." We nudge them socially, so they will "be accepted." We urge them vocationally, so they can "land a job." We may even spur them on athletically, so they can learn how "to compete." As fathers, however, how much do we do to truly equip our children spiritually?

How much do we strengthen and develop their souls, their relationship with God, and their resultant passion for life?

The "free spirits" we call *children* often become less free in their souls as they climb the maturity ladder we've placed in front of them. In America, we are good at urging them to "make the grade" or "leave their mark," but we also teach them how to conceal hurts, store bitterness, and not admit to their fears. In essence, we teach them how to close their souls and how to avoid and reject healthy opportunities to be honest, accepting, and open to spiritual direction.

Interestingly enough, while surrounded by dozens of adults eager to find out more about the kingdom of heaven, Jesus told them, "I tell you the truth, unless you change and become like little children, you will never enter the kingdom of heaven. Therefore, whoever humbles himself like this child is the greatest in the kingdom of heaven" (Matthew 18:3–4).

I find that when I allow my busy life and busied mind to slow down enough to focus on my kids—their view of the world and the state of their souls—I am always in for a blessing and, often, a lesson.

One day while riding into work, my mind riveted on what I had to do that day. Sitting next to me was my oldest daughter, Kristin, then about seven. As we made our way into town, she posed an unexpected question: "Dad, how old do you think we're all going to be in heaven?"

Fastened on my duties for the day, I responded, "Oh, I don't know, Kristin. Probably we're all going to be grown up—like adults—because by then we'll all be mature."

She grimaced in disbelief. "No, Dad. I don't think that's right."

"Well then, what do you think?" I ventured.

"Oh," she said with a confident smile, "I think you and me and everybody there are going to be kids, and we're going to run and play and sit on Jesus' lap."

You could smile at such sweetness and innocence. You could pat the little girl on the head and say, "That's cute."

But let me ask you, as a man, how *do* you relate to Jesus? How comfortable, at home, and free *are* you as a son of God? Are you duty-bound? Guilt-ridden? Feeling unacceptable? Resentful? A bit rebellious, wanting to run your life your way without God's "interference"? Or are you hurt or angry that God allowed some difficulty in your life?

Whatever is in your spirit *will* be communicated to your children in your words and attitudes. How much like you in spirit do you want your children to be?

And how *do* we go about rightly guiding their souls?

Out of the Mouths of Ten-Year-Olds

Children observe adults. And they form opinions.

One teacher polled her class of ten-year-olds as to their observations of grown-ups. Every child was given a chance to describe how they viewed adults. Here's what some of them said:

- "Grown-ups make promises and forget them. Or they say it was not really a promise, but a 'we'll see.' "
- "Grown-ups do not do the things they are always telling children to do, like picking up their things or speaking correctly or always telling the truth."
- "Whenever you ask 'why?' grown-ups always say dumb things like 'Because I said so,' or 'I'll explain later,' or 'I don't need a reason.' "
- "Grown-ups never listen to what children say and think they always have the right answer."
- "I am always being told not to interrupt people, but grown-ups interrupt children all the time."
- "I must say 'excuse me' whenever I burp. But when grown-ups burp they never say anything."
- "Grown-ups never admit when they're wrong, even if they know they are."
- "Grown-ups talk about money all the time. They say money is not important, but the way they talk about it, it must be."
- "Kids are not supposed to say mean things about each other, but grown-ups sit around and talk about each other that way all the time."
- "Grown-ups pry into children's secrets."
- "Grown-ups are always trying to prove something. They argue for a long time about the dumbest things."
- "Grown-ups always talk about what they did and what they knew when they were our age, but they never think about what it is like to be our age now."
- "Grown-ups almost never like to get silly. And when we have fun and get silly they always say, 'Settle down.' When they do get silly, it's the most fun we have."
- "Grown-ups make me sit around and be polite to the grown-ups, especially relatives, even though they are not polite or do not pay attention to me."
- "Grown-ups always tell you to eat only certain things, like vegetables and milk, but they eat whatever they want. They tell us not to waste food, but they throw away food all the time."

- "Sometimes grown-ups act like kids are invisible and talk about us like we're not there."
- "Grown-ups complain a lot. I love my birthday, but they always complain about being one year older when their birthdays happen."
- "I hope that when I grow up I'll remember what it was like being a kid."

Looking over this list, every honest man has to respond in one way—busted! These kids caught us at a host of hypocrisies, even those of us who consider ourselves to be spiritual men. Our actions speak so loudly our children cannot hear what we are saying.

If we will let down our defenses and rationalizations, there is much we men can learn from the observations of these youngsters. The things that seemed to get at them the most are not material in nature, but spiritual. Mull over this list carefully and ask yourself the question, "Do these adult tendencies open a child's soul to our guidance and direction or close it?"

The apostle Paul had a clear view of what it meant to be a father. He viewed the Christians in the various churches he planted as his spiritual "children." Without hesitation, Paul spoke often to his "children" about what God expected from them in their day-to-day behavior, about the rich inheritance they had in Christ, and about his heartfelt affection toward them.

When writing to the Thessalonian Christians, Paul described his home life among them and his fathering in this manner:

> You are witnesses, and so is God, of how holy, righteous and blameless we were among you who believed. For you know that we dealt with each of you as a father deals with his own children, encouraging, comforting and urging you to live lives worthy of God, who calls you into his kingdom and glory (1 Thessalonians 2:10–12).

Three words stand out: *encouraging, comforting* and *urging.* Three dynamics. Three influencing forces that flow from the heart of a godly father. Perhaps Paul had experienced these from his father in his own upbringing. Certainly, as a man he discovered their power and importance in the lives of those he was given to care for.

Encouragement: Crowning Your Kids

If you have never been to a Ukrainian or Greek wedding, you have truly missed a soul-moving experience. In these traditions there is a ritual that has accompanied wedding ceremonies for centuries. It is commonly referred to as the "crown ceremony." At a certain point in the wedding, the pastor or priest takes two beautiful crowns, and holding them above the couple's heads, he reminds them they are children of God. Because of that they are touched by the breath of divine royalty. They are challenged to love each other, and in faith and character to grow up into the crowns held above them. All the witnesses are committing themselves to encouraging this immature duo to grow up and be "crowned" with their titles—husband and wife, father and mother, man and woman, king and queen.

Talk about *encouragement!*

As the apostle Paul knew, encouragement is the act of inspiring others with renewed courage, spirit, or confidence. When we encourage our kids we spur them on; we give them hope, confidence, and affirmation. In this, it's important to remember the distinction between *appreciation* and *affirmation*. We appreciate what a person *does*, but we affirm who a person *is*. Affirmation stretches far beyond appreciation. Because appreciation focuses on a person's accomplishments, it carries with it a "price tag." A child can feel a pressure to produce in order to be appreciated. Affirmation runs deeper because it carriers no prerequisite. Even the child whose actions are not appreciated can still be affirmed. *In fact, he greatly needs to be affirmed.*

One communication expert has suggested that it takes ten postive words to offset the discouragement and pain of only one negative word. And there are some affirming things a dad might say—which every child needs to hear. Here are a few of my favorites:

"I'm glad I get to be your dad!"
"I sure love getting to spend time with you!"
"One of the things I like the best about you is . . ."
"I need a huge hug from you!"
"That was excellent. You do that really well!"
"We're buds, right?"
"You sure do look beautiful (handsome) today!"

Even as men, we hunger for a word of praise. Mark Twain is credited with saying, "I can live for two months on just one good compliment." All of us need affirmation and encouragement. And words that feed the soul are essential to small children and teenagers in their tedious growing, learning, and finding their footing in the world.

Danae Dobson expressed the impact her dad's encouragement has had on her life: "I knew I was special to him—that he was pulling for me and praying for me during each of the small crises that came my way. It's what every little girl needs from a father."

Genuine encouragement is food for the soul. Honest, supportive words of affirmation will bolster your children's spirits and inspire their sense of confidence. But withholding encouragement—because of anger, disgust, or as a form of punishment—disheartens and holds back children, dampening imagination and creativity. It can embitter, wound, and alienate a child from a parent.

Dreams and desires lie in the depths of every child's soul, and parental encouragement is the God-given force that can help set it free. Nothing else will do it as well. And silence will extinguish it.

The apostle Paul was careful to applaud not only Timothy's accomplishments but his person and character: "Timothy my true son in the faith . . ." (1 Timothy 1:2). "You, man of God . . ."(1 Timothy 6:11). "I have been reminded of your sincere faith" (2 Timothy 1:5). Paul learned how to praise people face-to-face, but he also learned to praise them "behind their backs," as he did when he wrote to the Philippians about Timothy: "I have no one else like him, who takes a genuine interest in your welfare. . . . But you know that Timothy has proved himself, because as a son with his father he has served with me in the work of the gospel" (Philippians 2:20, 22).

Comfort

From Paul, we learn that a second major aspect of spiritual fathering is giving *comfort* to our children. Comfort speaks of two things: first, providing noticeable support to our children during times of challenge; and second, offering reassurance in the midst of their apparent failures. Max Lucado sizes it up quite well:

> My child's feelings are hurt. I tell her she's special. My child is injured. I do whatever it takes to make her feel better. My child is afraid. I won't go to sleep until she is secure. I'm not a hero. I'm not a superstar. I'm not unusual. I'm a parent. When a child hurts, a parent does what comes naturally. He helps. And after I help, I don't charge a fee. I don't ask for a favor in return.
>
> You don't have to be a child psychologist to know that kids are "under construction." You don't have to have the wisdom of Solomon to realize that they didn't ask to be here in the first place, and that spilled milk can be wiped up and broken plates can be replaced.

Something tells me that in the whole scheme of things the tender moments described above are infinitely more valuable than anything I do in front of a computer screen or a congregation. Something tells me that the moments of comfort I give my child are a small price to pay for the joy of someday seeing my daughter do for her daughters what her dad did for her.[2]

The kind of comfort my three daughters and my son need must be deep, true, and constant. Sometimes I want to offer it like a faucet—on again, off again. They need something more dependable, words and acts of comfort that function like a well. They need to be able to draw upon my comfort whenever and wherever they need it. No, I cannot be with them every minute, but when I am with them I need to be *fully* with them. Not hidden behind a newspaper, distracted from their needs by the relentless beeper, or too busy with my own hobbies, sports, and escapes.

Gentle Urging

Paul knew the fatherly influence of *urging* children on in life. The word conjures up the image of a coach compelling his team on to victory. There is a force to the word that means, in essence, "strong discipline and direction." A man doesn't have to be a dad very long before he realizes that children don't know what is best for them. According to the Bible, kids come prepackaged with a bent toward foolish behavior because of sin: "Folly is bound up in the heart of a child, but the rod of discipline will drive it far from him" (Proverbs 22:15).

Children's misbehavior, at times, warrants carefully measured, restrained physical correction. But discipline goes far beyond physical correction. Discipline means instruction and training. The essence of the word implies that there is a leader in a child's life to provide modelling and clear direction.

Psalm 127:3–5 describes the role of a father as one who *aims* his children:

Sons are a heritage from the Lord,
    children a reward from him.
Like arrows in the hands of a warrior
    are sons born in one's youth.
Blessed is the man
    whose quiver is full of them.

Our world is sadly full of young adults who could be best described as *aimless.* Hollow eyes. Sterile souls. Passionless. Indecisive. Unfocused. Reluctant. What is needed most are fathers who will take the arrow of their children's souls and point them in the direction of the One who knows the plans that He has for them (see Jeremiah 29:11).

The process of bringing our children to God involves some tension and stretching, but if we fail to do so, our children will wander in spirit and more easily become caught up in the world's quagmire of disillusionment and pain.

Children need a father who will discipline them for their own sake—first by providing correction, and then by giving direction.

There are two ends to a shepherd's staff: One is straight, to nudge and prod in the right direction. The other is a crook, to draw them close and to hold them back. A faithful father learns how to do both with a strong spirit of love and devotion to his son or daughter.

Keeping Their Souls Open

My wife, Pamela, tells me that my influence in our kids' lives is unparalled. Ironic as it may seem, because she often spends more time with them than I in a given day, she says the fact, in her mind, is undeniable.

Not long ago, a study was conducted to discover how much influence a father has in the shaping of spiritual values in a child's life. The question was posed: "How many children are living as committed Christians at age twenty-five who were raised by a Christian mother and non-Christian father versus how many were raised with both parents knowing Christ?" The answer? Twenty-five percent were still Christians who only had a Christian mom. However, that number jumped to a whopping 75 percent when a believing father was added.

Bottom-line: Effective dads are Soul Openers. By prayer and practice they are learning to open their children up to their own influence, to God's will and His ways, and to the people in their lives. It is, after all, quite easy to tell when a child's soul is open or closed, isn't it? You can see it in the face, the tone, the body language, the attitude. I can walk into a room and quite easily tell whether my son's soul is open to me or closed. It's not difficult to see.

A shut-up soul is rigid and resistant. Whether by harsh words left unresolved or parental neglect, a closed soul is evident when our kids no longer naturally look us in the eye. When a son or daughter avoids engaging Dad in dialogue or eye-contract, something's wrong. Of course, there are those times of brooding that follow seasons of correction and discipline in which conversation is tough. However, such seasons should not be simply abandoned. These times need to be followed up with reaffirming words of love, with a prayer, an embrace. Confrontations always need some sort of closure. A moment that says to a child's soul: "We are going to move beyond this, love each other, and grow from it. Most of all, I want you to know that I love you."

So, how is a dad to keep the soul of his child open? What are the ingredients that go into not only living from the soul, but helping our children to do the same? God has, in fact, given us at least five fatherly tools of influence that can work wonders in opening our sons and daughters up to God—and ourselves, for that matter.

SOUL OPENER #1

The Moments You Make

Even mud can make a moment. I found that out when my daughter was about three. Swimming in the ocean, I reached into the water and scooped up some sand beneath the surface. Taking the mud, I smeared it on my arm and said, "Kristin, do you know what this looks like?" She shook her head "no." "That's what sin looks like in our hearts," I returned. Her eyes widened. "And, do you know what Jesus' blood does?" As her head shook again, I plunged my arm deep into the water and brought it up just as quick, saying, "It washes it all away." She was instantly hooked. She insisted that I repeat the process at least a dozen times that day.

It has been years since I gave Kristin that object lesson. And yet, not many months back I observed her, now twelve, doing the exact same story with my four-year-old son, Robbi.

Life is full of teachable moments just waiting to be captured. The key essential is: BE SPONTANEOUS.

SOUL OPENER #2

The Promises You Keep

Kids need someone they can count on. Whenever I make my son or daughter a promise, I touch their soul. How? Well, when I make a promise, I immediately place hope within them. Hope is a sacred thing. It is a motivator. As a matter of fact, hope is the one thing none of us can live without. It is forceful and irresistible.

When I break a promise the results can be soul-stripping. Consider this verse: "Hope deferred makes the heart sick, but a promise fulfilled is a tree of life" (Proverbs 13:12, KJV).

The challenge I face is: BE CONSISTENT. Whenever I faithfully keep a promise, regardless of the cost, the results can be soul-enlivening ("a tree of life"). A "promise fulfilled" builds a bridge not only into my child's life but into their soul. Not only does it encourage my son or daughter, it strengthens our relationship and paves a path for them toward a God who never fails to keep a promise.

SOUL OPENER #3

The Questions You Ask

The one thing none of us can resist is genuine interest. Years ago, Dale Carnegie captured the principle in these words: "In order to be interesting, you must be interested. You will gain more friends in three minutes by getting interested in others than you will in three months of trying to get them interested in you." Everyone loves to be asked about themselves, especially kids.

One of the most overlooked and underused tools in a parent's toolbox is great questions.[3] A while back, one of my friends picked up his eleven-year-old daughter at school. Wanting to strike up a conversation, he asked, "So, how was school today?" "Okay," his daughter responded. And that was it. The car became tensely quiet (know the feeling?). The question, intended to engage her and create interest, fell far short. I have known similar moments.

The problem was that the question was not sharp enough. It was flat and unfocused. After some encouragement, my buddy gave it another shot. "So, what was the best thing that happened to you all day?" According to my friend, that sharpened question struck gold. He and his daughter talked all the way home, and then some.

Talkshow hosts spend hours sharpening questions in order to effectively engage the people they interview. Doesn't it make sense for us dads to give some thought to what we're asking our kids and to how we're going about it? The motivating key: BE INTERESTED. It's downright irresistible.

Remember, a good question can open a conversation; a great one can open a soul.

Soul Opener #4

The Insights You Impart

"What we have heard and known, what our fathers have told us. We will not hide them from their children; we will tell the next generation the praiseworthy deeds of the Lord, his power, and the wonders he has done" (Psalm 78:3–4).

The sayings of a father. That is in essence what comprises the majority of the book of Proverbs. Hundreds of succinct statements of faith, value, and conviction that Solomon used to pepper the souls of his sons in order to teach them the ways of wisdom.

My mind frequently swells with memories of the faithful sayings my dad seasoned my own soul with:

"Robert, remember—always think before you speak."

"Your grandfather kept the Crosby name good. I've tried to do the same. I expect you to do the same while you are away on this trip. It is up to you to keep a good name."

"Any job worth doing is worth doing right."

"Many a man has lost his soul over not controlling his sex drive."

"When you start this job, remember: delegate, delegate, delegate. Don't try to do it all on your own."

Nothing can take the place of the insights of a father. God has designed the hearts of sons and daughters in such a way that they are incredibly influenced by the convictions of their dad. The wise father understands that in order to raise faithful sons and daughters, he must BE DEVOTED to each of them. He must pass on the nuggets of wisdom and insight he has learned. A "good provider" puts more than food on the table, he plants wisdom in the heart.

SOUL OPENER #5

The Time You Take

To make the most of a moment takes time, an investment of our lives and energy. Without a doubt, saying yes to time with our kids means saying no to some of the time we spend with other aspects of our lives— our job, our hobbies, sitting in front of the TV. Just this morning I shared breakfast with a man who is working in a job that is significantly below his qualifications. He could, in fact, have a job that paid more and did more to build his resumé. He could have a more impressive office, title, expense account. He has chosen, however, to say no to that. Why? In his words:

> In the job I am currently in, I am free to set my own schedule as long as I get the job done. So, my boss is comfortable with me leaving in the afternoon to attend my son's ball games or to leave the office early if my wife needs my help. The promotions I could pursue would never allow me that. Sure, I get paid less because of it . . . but, in ways that count, I am really paid more.

That is a dad who has made time with his kids a literal priority. Oh, yes, I know that not all of us can find such a role, but certainly we can all make time. If my job says, "To do me well, you can't have a family life," then I need to rethink my role, my goals, my standard of living, and my priorities. After all, "What does it profit a man if he gains the whole world and loses his own soul?" . . . or his son or daughter?

What kids need most from their dads is time with them. In a word, for them to BE THERE!

MORE SOUL OPENERS

Twenty Ways to Draw Closer to Your Kids

1. Look your son or daughter in the eye and tell him or her sincerely, "I'm so glad that *I* get to be *your* dad!"

2. While riding in the car with them, reach over and hold their hand or put your arm around their shoulder, for no other reason than to show your love for them.

3. Before you drop them off at school or at a friend's house for the

night, ask to say a prayer with them.

4. When they go to bed at night, take your son by the hand and pray that he'll grow up to be a man of God. Take your daughter by the hand and pray that she'll grow up to be a woman of God.

5. If you see a discouraged or disappointed look on your child's face, ask if they need a hug. Then give them a good one!

6. Take your daughter or son out to a restaurant alone with you. Ask what *they* would like to talk about. Set no limits as to the subject. Let them order whatever they would like to eat.

7. When your son or daughter has something they're eager to tell you about, listen with interest—with eye focus. Discipline yourself to be concerned about what concerns them.

8. Get on the floor and wrestle with your kids.

9. Try to remember something you experienced when you were your child's age. Take some time to tell them about it. Invite their questions as well.

10. When your own parents are over visiting, invite your kids to ask them whatever they want to know about what you were like when you were a child. You can moderate the questions and answers.

11. When you have been overly harsh with your children, be man enough to ask for their forgiveness. Close this time with prayer. Allow your child to hear you asking God's forgiveness. Charles Stanley has said that when a dad admits to his children that he was wrong and is in need of forgiveness, he sits down "six-feet tall" and stands up "ten-feet tall."

12. When your child fails in a sports event or other activity, assure him or her that this is only human. There is no reason to be ashamed.

13. Before your child picks up his lunchbox or school books on the way out the door, slip a note inside. Write something encouraging, such as, "I hope your day is terrific! Don't forget, Dad is praying for you. Lots of love . . ."

14. Don't only commend appropriate actions in your children, learn to affirm godly characteristics, too. For instance, when your child takes out the garbage the first time he's asked, you could say, "It was great to see you obey right away without hesitation. Thanks."

15. When your child says she is afraid of the dark, instead of scolding her or shaming her, go to her room with her, sit by her bedside and ask what she is specifically afraid of. You could then read some Scripture verses about fear, or tell her about a time when you were afraid as a child. Then pray with her.

16. Make it a goal to discover one thing your son/daughter has a

knack for or special interest in. Invest some time, effort, and resources to encourage growth in this area.

17. Instead of flipping through graded homework quickly, sit down and take the time to comment on it. Affirm successes. Acknowledge errors. Encourage development.

18. When your child is unusually irritable, instead of taking it as an affront to your leadership, scope it out further. Sit down and ask what the trouble is, and what you can do to help.

19. Invite your child to join you on a hike or long walk. Bring along a pocket New Testament. Along the way, stop and read an appropriate passage and talk to them about it. Encourage them to share their dreams. Pray together.

20. When your son or daughter reaches fifteen or sixteen, take them out for a snack or a meal at a restaurant. A week or so beforehand, tell them you want to devote the evening to talking about the kind of person they would like to marry someday. Keep it light and fun, not heavy and probing. During your conversation, discover what characteristics are important to them, and what they will look for in a mate. Make a list together. Take some time to talk about the characteristics you appreciate most in your spouse. Then promise to pray with your child regarding this important subject, and encourage them to talk to you about any questions or problems they may confront in the future regarding dating or serious friendships.

Notes

1. As quoted in *Along the Road to Manhood*, by Stu Weber (Multnomah, 1995), p. 57.
2. Max Lucado, *The Applause of Heaven* (Word Publishing, 1990), p. 62.
3. Robert Crosby has two books on asking great questions entitled: *Now We're Talking! Questions to Build Intimacy With Your Spouse* and *Now We're Talking! Questions That Bring You Closer to Your Kids* (Focus on the Family Publishing).

CHAPTER TWELVE

Leading Your Household to God

"These commandments that I give you today are to be upon your hearts. Impress them on your children. Talk about them when you sit at home and when you walk along the road, when you lie down and when you get up."

Deuteronomy 6:6–7

"A father's number one priority . . . is to communicate the real meaning of Christianity to his children."

—Dr. James Dobson

Family Devotions

What comes to mind when you think of family devotions? Reluctance or eagerness? Frustration or encouragement? Guilt or confidence?

If you're like most Christian men, the thought of personal devotions is challenging enough. But few things conjure up frustration like the thought of family devotions. Many men feel they *should* be leading their family in a regular diet of spiritual nourishment, that they *should* have a consistent time in which their wife and children are strengthened in their faith. But most often, we just don't know where to begin—or if we do begin, how to continue.

Here are a few reasons or excuses people give for not beginning a regular family devotional time:

- "We just don't seem to have the time."
- "We go to church. Why do we need family devotions?"

- "We have toddlers in our home. They're too rambunctious to sit through devotions."
- "We have teenagers in our home. Their schedules don't allow for family devotions."
- "I've never been to Bible college or seminary. I don't feel qualified to teach the Bible."
- "Our kids' ages are too spread out. What would interest our youngest would never interest our oldest."

But the biggest roadblocks that keep us from initiating meaningful family devotional times are our own misconceptions, apprehensions, and insecurities.

In my first few years as a father, I often felt the need to initiate a devotional time, but I kept coming up short in the confidence department. It wasn't so much a lack of knowledge as a host of wrong ideas or misconceptions, all of which served to weaken my motivation.

Men's Misconceptions About Family Devotions

Misconception #1: *Family devotions have to be led like a standard church service. There has to be an opening prayer, some singing and then a message, followed by another prayer.*

Who says? This idea is more traditional than biblical. Jesus certainly was not bound by a rigid structure in discipling the Twelve. He incorporated dozens of diverse object lessons and teaching tools to inspire and equip them. He generally preferred a parable from everyday life over a podium and a lecture. He usually chose a good story over a course in systematic theology.

Every dad can do the same. The ways you instruct your family in their faith should be simple—the simpler and more commonplace the better.

Misconception #2: *Everybody has to sit still and be quiet for family devotion times in order for them to be really effective. Still* and *quiet* are not synonymous with *toddlers* or *teenagers.* Although it's important to cultivate attentiveness and respect in children when others are speaking, my experience has been that stillness is not something kids are pre-programmed with. Attentiveness is learned, and it takes time and tons of patience to teach it!

Little children, by nature, are tactile. They want to engage everyone around them in conversation. They want to touch and experience life. The best learning experiences inspire children to consider truth and understand how to make it part of their lives.

In the gospel of Mark, a group of rowdy children were clamoring to get close enough to touch Jesus, perhaps to sit in His lap. The disciples saw the children's behavior as inappropriate and bothersome. Jesus saw it as an irresistible invitation to influence their lives and shape their souls. He said:

> "Let the little children come to me, and do not hinder them, for the kingdom of God belongs to such as these. I tell you the truth, anyone who will not receive the kingdom of God like a little child will never enter it." And he took the children in his arms, put his hands on them and blessed them (Mark 10:14–16).

Encourage your children to "come to Jesus" with all their concerns, fears, disappointments, irritations, and needs. Don't "parent" them as the disciples did by censoring their feelings, prayers, or questions.

Don't say to a child who feels sad at the death of a grandparent, "God doesn't want you to feel sad. Grandma is with God now." Rather, tell him or her, "God wants you to talk to Him and tell Him how you are feeling. Ask Him to comfort you during this hard time. I'm sad and miss Grandma too." Put your arms around your child and comfort him or her with your presence.

Misconception #3: *The spouse who knows the most Scripture should give the spiritual instruction.* Many Christian fathers became believers after their wives did. As a result, the thought of leading devotions or teaching their families is a scary thought. They may feel they come up short in the area of biblical knowledge, especially in comparison with their wives.

But the thing that qualifies us to lead our families spiritually is not the extent of our personal knowledge of the Bible. It's our personal commitment to Christ and the fact that God has made us the spiritual leader of our home. Growing in our understanding of the Bible will enhance our knowledge of God. We can learn and grow with our family.

Misconception #4: *Telling Bible stories to kids is a woman's job.* No . . . it's a *parent's* job. If a father leaves this duty to his wife, his kids will grow up believing that spiritual matters aren't that important to men. Children need to see the personal commitment their father has to the Word of God.

Misconception #5: *If one of the kids misbehaves during devotions, it will ruin the whole thing.*

We cannot wait for our children to become "perfect angels" before we engage their impressionable minds and lives in His Word. Family devotions are not rigid rituals to be endured, but lively interchanges of truth, grace, and life to be enjoyed in their truest sense.

In our home, when it's time for sharing and learning in a devotional setting, it is easy to read the frame of mind the kids are in. They show it in their demeanor and body language. Instead of showing a posture of interest, sometimes the shoulders are slouched or the lips are pooched, communicating loud and clear—"I don't want to be here." As a man, a part of me immediately wants to react, to scold and criticize. At times I have done just that. When I have, however, my irritability becomes the final straw that ruins the mood.

But when I have carefully and lovingly engaged the conflict with a question or two, the process has often had a way of turning the resistance into an invitation . . . to teach and to train.

After all, we determine to have family devotions as a family because we want to become more truly Christian in the way we live. For that to happen, the "sins" in our midst must rise to the surface as we draw closer together. Whether it's sibling rivalry, unforgiveness, anger, disappointment, envy, or whatever, the sin symptoms reveal just where God's truth needs to be targeted. The conflicts don't have to destroy family devotions. In fact, they can more accurately "aim" us toward genuine needs.

Misconception #6: *Devotions should mainly involve reading the Bible together.*

The first time Pam and I ever sat down with our firstborn two-year-old to share in devotions, I was determined that it was going to work. My "plan" was that we would begin with Genesis 1:1 and read through the Bible together. (Over time, of course.) There I was, sitting at the kitchen table ready to launch this process—with my wife, my beautiful little daughter, and my Bible. What else did we need?

Pam had her doubts about the idea. But I plunged ahead.

About halfway through the first verse, Kristin started making one of those playful sounds that toddlers make. I responded, "Now, sweetie, you have to be quiet so Dad can read. Here we go." No sooner had I begun to read than she had come up with another sound, this time louder. "Kristin Anne, be quiet so Dad can read. We are having family devotions!" I asserted.

But this was not her idea of a fun time. Between Kristin's sound effects and my retorts, the tension escalated.

Within five minutes, I felt a complete failure at family devotions and was ready to throw in the towel and go watch "Jeopardy."

We soon discovered that in order to get our little girl involved and interested in family devotions I would have to do much more than merely engage her ears. I not only had to read the passage, I had to act it, sing it—you name it! Her eager eyes, inquisitive mind, and moldable spirit needed something more than holy intonations.

Misconception #7: *The best devotions can only occur when the whole family is together.*

I used to believe this, until we went from two children in the circle to four. Recently, Pam and I recognized that, with the addition of a three-year-old and a six-month-old, our approach to family devotions was changing without our recognizing it. Although we had added new learning techniques and approaches as our two oldest daughters approached adolescence, we were now finding ourselves reverting to old patterns because of the attention demands of our little ones. Up to that point, we'd assumed that family devotions had to include the whole family together for the whole time. Frustrated and a bit frazzled, we decided to try something different.

To deal with our dilemma, we set up a ten-minute, to-the-point devotional time with everyone involved and asked the older girls to bear with us while we made it the best it could be for Robbi. After that segment, we put the two younger ones to bed and then continued for another half-hour or so in interactive Bible study with our older children.

Much to our delight, it worked! Our toddler was told a Bible story the way he likes it while the girls helped us teach. Then, our daughters were able to share in a much-needed look at God's Word and the issues facing them in life.

Misconception #8: *Parents should always teach, and children should always listen.* Jesus made it clear that children could teach adults much about humility and responsiveness to God. Often, in our devotional times, we have found the best instruction has come not from the pages of our study notes, but straight from the hearts of our children.

Although parents should do most of the teaching, don't underestimate the insights that can spring from your children as you allow them to share. They are seldom boring and often disarmingly honest.

Misconception #9: *The best time for devotions is right before the kids go to bed.*

Not all Bible stories are bedtime stories. Certainly there is something special about praying with our children when they go to bed. But often we choose "bedtime stories" in hopes that reading will put them to sleep! Keep in mind that some Bible stories really call for the kids to be alert and attentive.

Choose the time when you think your children will absorb the most.

Misconception #10: *Dad must always lead the devotional time.*

This is not necessary, but Dad should be sure that someone leads it regularly. The key is to have a plan, develop it, and stick with it. There may be times when you are overloaded at work and you ask your wife to lead devotions. You may choose to rotate leading with your wife. You may even ask one of your kids to lead in singing or tell a Bible story. However you can get family members to participate is a plus for the overall experience of learning and studying God's Word.

Essentials for Dynamite Devotions

The following essentials have freed me up as a dad to not only lead devotional times, but to genuinely enjoy doing so.

Essential #1: *A father who regularly initiates devotional times with his family.*

The best gift you can give your children is to regularly bring God to them through Bible reading and prayer, and regularly bring them closer to God by helping them to participate in family devotions.

Essential #2: *The central goal of family devotions is to impress God, His Word, and His ways upon the souls of your children.*

In speaking of the commandment to love God, the Lord himself instructs parents, "These commandments that I give you today are to be upon your hearts. Impress them on your children. Talk about them when you sit at home and when you walk along the road, when you lie down and when you get up" (Deut. 6:6–7). Parenting includes far more than imparting information. It involves shaping souls.

Essential #3: *For family devotions to work, ground rules must be established.*

We regularly emphasize to our kids what is required of them to make our family devotion time the best it can be. A few of our ground rules include:

- After having been corrected once, if you continue to disrupt the devotional time, you will be disciplined and will not share with the family in the remainder of it.

- When someone else is talking, we will focus our eyes and attention upon that person.
- You can ask any question you would like to ask as long as you speak in turn.
- If your attitude communicates disinterest or a repeated unwillingness to cooperate, you will be disciplined and not share in the remainder.

Essential #4: *Keep it simple.*

Trying to cover too much material or too many subjects in one sitting is overkill. The kids won't retain it all and will lose interest early.

For example, if you are walking together through the life of a Bible character, don't rush it or try to cover too much in one evening. One key focal point, event, or principle is enough for one sitting. Establish a clear goal in advance: exactly what you want to drive home to your children. Break the principle down to its simplest level and try expressing it in various interesting ways.

Essential #5: *Make it interesting. Communicate excitement.*

One devoted-to-devotions dad suggests: "Try not to say things like: 'You will not get out of that chair until we are through'; 'Be quiet and listen'; 'One more giggle out of you and you'll go to your room!' Rather, reinforce a positive attitude by saying something like: 'Guess who we're going to meet in the Bible tonight?'; 'Let's have a contest. . . .' 'I'm really excited about the Bible passage we're going to read tonight.' "

Don't just try to bring your toddler or teenager into the world of Elijah (or whatever Bible character you're studying)—bring Elijah into *their* world. (For assistance in putting together a Bible study for your children on your own, see the section at the end of this chapter, entitled "Making It P.L.A.I.N.")

Essential #6: *Make prayer together a family priority.*

Family devotions are truly devotions when time is spent devoting heart and life to God. Our children need to hear us talking to God about their souls. They must become familiar with bringing hurts and hopes, plans and problems, praise and adoration before the throne of God. Whether kneeling together, standing, or holding hands, varying the postures of prayer can be very meaningful. One beautiful form of prayer is for everyone in the family to lay their hands on the back, shoulders, or head of a family member who is sick or in special need.

Essential #7: *Look for "teachable moments."*

Parents who desire to disciple their children do so best by learning to be alert to "teachable moments." Almost any setting is appropriate for nurturing and training a child. Jesus taught in temples, on beaches, in homes, on boats, at breakfast, at weddings, at wells, on mountains . . . even on the cross. In short, everywhere He went.

An unexpected thunderstorm provided a ready-made object lesson for me just a few weeks ago with my four kids. Amidst the unfamiliar claps of thunder and the strobe-shots of lightning, I turned off the television and the lights and instructed them to follow me upstairs. Finding the window with the best view we all sat together still and quiet and listened closely. A few questions seemed appropriate: Isn't it amazing how powerful God must be? How does this thunderstorm make you feel? What does this display tell you about what God must be like? What do you see out there? What do you hear?

A hundred-page book or a two-hour movie could not have evoked the sense of awe that just a few minutes under God's creation did. The teachable moment was there. Ripe. Powerful. Ready to be captured. All it took was a little spontaneity on my part. The result was a wonderful sense of closeness to God and one another. I wish I could say that I thought of it myself, but the fact is my mother did the same thing with me during the South Carolina thunderstorms I grew up under. I wonder if her mom or dad did the same with her. Life is full of opportunities to teach our children, if we watch for them.

Essential #8: *Ask great questions.*

The kinds of questions you ask your children during your devotional time is a big factor in making the time fascinating.

For example, if you were doing a Bible study on Elijah, which of these sample questions would draw the most out of your child?

1. What did you think about the story?

2. At times, Elijah had to stand alone in order to stand for God. What does it take for you to stand up for God at school? Do you ever feel like you are standing alone? In what ways?

Taking the time to consider *what* you will ask your child and *how* you will ask it is vital to any meaningful devotional time. Ask questions that cannot be answered with a mere yes or no. Ask questions that are focused and that draw upon your child's feelings, insights, and impressions.

Essential #9: *Give lessons on their level—speak from God's Word to the issues of their lives.*

Anyone can read verbatim from the Bible or a devotional book. It takes a resourceful parent to personalize the truth to the lives of their children. Guard against empty recitation and obligatory response. In order to fully engage the mind and soul of my children, I must be tuned into their needs.

Essential #10: *Demonstrate. Demonstrate. Demonstrate.*

Impromptu drama has been the most effective tool we have used as a family to apply spiritual truth. Drama completely absorbs their minds, bodies, and emotions, and it gets everyone involved. It is the one learning tool that I have never seen our children become bored with.

One of our kids' favorite stories to dramatize is the temptation of Jesus in the wilderness. Someone plays the role of Jesus, someone acts out the devil's part, and someone portrays the angel who came to feed Jesus after the forty-day fast. Having familiarized myself with the story ahead of time, I sometimes find it best to *tell* it rather than read it. Then I give the kids their lines as they occur in the story, and they repeat after me until they get it down.

You don't need elaborate props. Use whatever is handy and lots of imagination. By the end of the story, the kids are ready to do it over again.

Object lessons are great learning tools, as well. Max Lucado tells of the time he was teaching his children about the way God provided food for the people of Israel when they were traveling to the Promised Land. In order to demonstrate God's provision, Max placed pieces of crackers on the ceiling fan blades ahead of time. At the right moment in the story, he turned on the fan and "manna" fell from heaven, much to the surprise of the children. Ordinary things can become great tools for teaching extraordinary principles.

Music talks are an excellent way to bring God's Word into your teenager's life. This can be done by playing a selected contemporary Christian song from a tape or CD. Then discuss what the lyrics mean and look at related Bible verses.

Essential #11: *Live out the lesson. Teach your children to minister to one another. Provide opportunities for them to do what they are being taught.*

One of the best ways to teach truth is to provide a setting where your children can *do* what they're learning. At times, we ask one of our children, in advance, to lead the singing time. We ask another to tell us one of their favorite Bible stories, and another to bring a Christian song for us to listen to and discuss.

Some have found it beneficial to take their family to a nursing home or the children's ward of a hospital, where they can learn to demonstrate love to others.

Essential #12: *Ritual brings truth to life and speaks to every generation.*

We have implemented a few "rituals" into our family devotions around holiday times that have been powerful tools for communicating truth.

Two of our favorites include: an Advent wreath experience throughout December and an at-home Seder (Passover meal) at Eastertime, with all the items on the table to represent Jesus' Last Supper. There is something powerfully bonding about coming together around vivid and symbolic Christian rituals such as these. Our kids tend to remember these worship and learning experiences and to look forward to them each year.

Give yourself freedom to try new methods.

The most difficult aspect of having family devotions is getting started. The enemy of your soul will provide many reasons and diversions—if you allow him—to keep you from doing what you know you need to do. But once you start, in partnership with your spouse (if possible), give it your best shot and you're off and running! The keys to continuing are to avoid getting into ruts, to stay sensitive to the changing needs and attention capabilities of your children, and to give yourself the space to try new things. Some of them will work, while others won't.

Take some time each week to pray and prepare what you will share. Make the time you've set aside a priority. Single out a night each week as Family Night and keep it sacred. Guard it passionately! Ask God to guide you as to how you should nurture and lead your home flock. I'm convinced He is eager to do so.

If you're devoted to the goal of bringing God into your home and leading your family closer to Him, you're halfway there. If you're convinced devotions are needed in your home, then step out and initiate them.

Why not this week?

Soul Opener

Make It P.L.A.I.N.

How to make a Bible story or passage interesting and understandable for your children!

Can you put together a simple Bible study for your children? What does it take? In the following you will find a simple guide to help you teach a Bible story creatively to your kids. Make it plain!

Picture the prophet in tennis shoes.

Imagine what this particular Bible character's faith adventure would have been like if he had to live it out in the world and setting your child faces today (i.e., neighborhood, school, church).

List the key principles/insights.

What are the major principles and insights for life that you can draw from this passage/story for your child? Write them down so you can pass them on.

Activate the insights. Get everyone involved.

Consider ways in which your child can demonstrate these valuable lessons from the Bible via drama, discussion, craftmaking, music, drawing, construction, etc.

Illustrate! Illustrate! Illustrate!

What stories have you heard or experienced in life that would illustrate this particular principle to your child? Tell them these stories.

Never bore!

I believe it was D. L. Moody who said, "It is a sin to make this glorious gospel boring."

PART FOUR

A Supported Soul
(The Man God *Uses!*)

CHAPTER THIRTEEN

"Am I My Brother's Keeper?"

"There was a man all alone; he had neither son nor brother. There was no end to his toil."

Ecclesiastes 4:8

"Once we open our world to another man, we learn that we are not alone in our fears, insecurities, uncertainties, and desires. . . . Through friendship with another man, we affirm much of what is good and strong in us as men. Frank and honest exchanges of experiences allow us to gain a fresh and clear perspective on ourselves."

—Dr. Ken Druck, *The Secrets Men Keep*

Most men I know are running low on passion, that soul fuel that makes life worth living.

Our inability to connect with our world shows up on elevators as clearly as anywhere. Surely you've experienced it.

Adults file onto a crowded elevator and immediately observe "The Unwritten Rules of Elevator Riding."

Rule Number One: *Do not look at anyone else while on the elevator.* Eye contact is strictly forbidden—especially with another man. If you must look somewhere, look at your shoe tops.

Rule Number Two: *Absolutely no talking with other passengers.* Everyone must maintain a vigil of silence. All noises—including sneezing, coughing, laughing, humming—makes things uncomfortable.

Rule Number Three: *Do not get any closer to the other passengers than you have to.* Keep as much space between you and others as possible. For example, if there are only two of you aboard, stand in opposite corners like prizefighters.

Elevator rides tell us a lot about men when they find themselves at close range with others. We're awkward. Uncomfortable. Confident men can lose all sense of confidence when they have to be close and interactive with other men.

But let a child look you in the eye, or unexpectedly grab your hand in a crowd, and you smile. You wink. You reassure with a look.

The open face of a child makes us feel—what is it? *Welcomed.* A child's face rolls out a red carpet for weary souls and on-edge adults. It says to us, "Relax. Everything's okay. You're here, I'm here, and that's just great!" Such an experience is at once a blessing . . . and an *indictment.*

What we find in the face of a child is what we have forgotten how to find in one another as adults—as men. For the eyes of our peers often threaten us. Another man's steady gaze seems to say, "Just who do you think you are? And what are you thinking about me?"

Shielded. Guarded. Protected. Most men tend to live in such a manner. Our culture teaches us to cover up our inner life. We keep our dreams, uncertainties, hopes, disappointments, and fears to ourselves. We do so to shield our souls from others.

And all the while, within us is a deep need to live life differently. To know and be known by other men.

Rod Cooper defines intimacy as "the ability to experience an open, supportive, compassionate relationship with another person without the fear of condemnation or the loss of one's identity. It is knowing another person deeply and appreciating them anyway."[1] Intimacy is not only for a male/female romantic relationship. It is for men who will never be free from their fear of inadequacy, never free from secret sins, until another man who knows him well shows him how to reconnect with God in the inner being. Intimacy can be a courageous closeness in relationship to another man. This intimacy challenges and builds the soul.

Men desperately need to experience openness and honesty with God, with their spouses, *and* with other men. In order to effectively learn how to live life from the soul, a man must consistently and intentionally have times in his life when he lays down his shield and armor and reveals what's inside himself to a friend, a brother, a spiritual comrade. Some believe it is this fear that another will see what is going on inside that makes men so uncomfortable to be looked in the eye by another man.

The Friendships of Men

The result of our cultural grooming, however, is that many men do not have even one close male friend. Men have to struggle to go beyond having mere acquaintances.

In her book *The Friendships of Women*, Dee Brestin sizes up the situation quite well:

> Studies indicate that men, like boys, *do* things together—Rotary, softball, hunting—but they do not often relate to each other as confidants. Men tend to be side by side, engrossed in an activity, whereas women will be face-to-face. Men may confuse quantity of time spent in the company of other men with intimacy. Most men not only find it difficult to make themselves vulnerable to each other, but they are often uncomfortable being together unless their attention can be centered on activity.[2]

"I envy the women in this church!" Roy's words captured my attention. Just entering my first year of senior pastoring, I was having lunch with this young father and husband to get his interpretation of some of the greatest needs facing our church family. "They have a spiritual connection that the men don't have," he observed.

"How so?" I asked.

"When the women greet each other you can tell they genuinely know and care about each other. I wish the men had that kind of connection. Right now we relate on a pretty shallow level."

Another man, a columnist for *The Washington Post*, sized up the painful shallowness of our man-to-man relationships in this way:

> My friends have no friends. They are men. They think they have friends, and if you ask them whether they have friends they will say yes, but they don't really. They think, for instance, that I'm their friend, but I'm not. It's okay. They're not my friends either.
>
> The reason for that is that we are all men—and men, I have come to believe, cannot or will not have real friends. They have something else—companions, buddies, pals, chums, someone to drink with and someone to wrench with and someone to lunch with, but no one when it comes to saying how they feel—especially how they hurt. . . . Women will tell you all the time they don't know the men they live with. They talk of long silences and drifting off and of keeping feelings

hidden and never letting on that they are troubled or bothered or whatever.

If it's any comfort to women, they should know it's nothing personal. Men treat other men the same way.[3]

Getting Over the Hurdles

The greatest obstacle a man faces to experiencing real openness is a naturally competitive nature. The drive to compete hinders men from building Christ-honoring and soul-enriching relationships with other men in several ways.

First, competitiveness compels a man to work at getting other people interested in himself.

It is a sad thing to watch a grown man working overtime to impress others or to gain a greater sense of significance—sadder still when you catch yourself doing so. This tendency is opposite the life principle Paul promoted: "Each of you should look not only to your own interests, but also to the interests of others" (Philippians 2:4).

George W. Morgan sized it up well: "Our social fabric militates against [relationship]. Competitiveness pervades everything we do and is taught from the time we are small children. Work and play are conceived of as contest and race. . . . We seize on the half-truth that competiion forces everyone to do his best . . . and completely ignore what this does to human [relationships]. Our fundamental stance is not to respond to others, but to out-do them, vie with them, beat them."

Second, competitiveness causes a man to avoid the admission of weakness or failure at all costs.

Given our innate drive to compete socially rather than connect spiritually, men become experts at isolation and denial. It is as if we say to other men, "If I connect with you, you may see a weakness. And I don't want you to see my weakness, because then you'll use it to beat me." The result? In the name of appearing "strong," we often lack the courage to face our own weaknesses, to be honest about the dark side.

Third, competitiveness keeps the conversations of men shallow, temporal, and impersonal.

We men become adept at raising smoke screens and force fields around us. Why is it that we can talk to one another about the rough weather we've been having but not about "storms" in our own marriage and fathering experience? And what is it about us that finds it so easy to discuss the ups and downs of our favorite ball team or the stock market, and never a word about the highs and lows of our dreams and fears? In a word, *competitiveness*.

We Don't Even Know Ourselves

Another major obstacle to developing supportive, open friendships is our personal *blindness*.

You see, others can often see in us what we refuse to see in ourselves. The angry man, the manipulator, the self-pitier—most men can see these traits in us a mile off, and they tend to back away.

No one can help us come to know ourselves the way God can—if we open ourselves to Him in prayer. *We need this help.* A serious lack of self-knowledge can lead to untold misery and a life of isolation.

Consider what happened to Cain. The Bible gives us his sad story:

> Abel kept flocks, and Cain worked the soil. In the course of time Cain brought some of the fruits of the soil as an offering to the Lord. But Abel brought fat portions from some of the firstborn of his flock. The Lord looked with favor on Abel and his offering, but on Cain and his offering he did not look with favor. So Cain was very angry, and his face was downcast.
>
> Then the Lord said to Cain, "Why are you so angry? Why is your face downcast? If you do what is right, will you not be accepted? But if you do not do what is right, sin is crouching at your door; it desires to have you, but you must master it" (Genesis 4:2–7).

Two short paragraphs into the story and the plot is already sin-thick. Two brothers, wired differently. Both worship the same God. As an offering, one brings "some of the fruits" of his labor. The other, "some of the *firstborn* of his flock." More than an offering, Abel brings a sacrifice.

When God confronts Cain, you get the feeling He's trying to show him the contents of his own soul.

God's words cut to the heart:

"Why are you so angry?" (His gaze doesn't miss a single soul-symptom.)

"Why is your face so downcast?" (He is concerned about Cain's disappointment and hurt—the real fuel of his anger.)

"If you do what is right, will you not be accepted?" (He sizes up the real issue and reaches out to fill the true need of Cain's soul.)

"But if you do not do what is right, sin is crouching at your door; it desires to have you, but you must master it."

God observed more than an expression; He perceived a thought and the spirit behind it (cf. Psalm 139:2, 23–24). God knows that acts of rebellion start out as seeds of discontent.

Here's the issue: temptation plays upon the rebel concealed within everyone of us. As James says,

> But each one is tempted when, by his own evil desire, he is dragged away and enticed. Then, after desire has conceived, it gives birth to sin; and sin, when it is full-grown, gives birth to death (1:14–15).

You'd think that a one-on-one dialogue with God would be enough to show him his heart motives. But it seems we men are masters at playing hide-and-seek: Cain had a perfect chance to admit the terrible thoughts lurking in him. Instead he hid them—and went away to brood.

In time, Cain's hidden anger warped his soul so badly that he murdered his own brother. Instead of letting God open his stubborn soul and cleanse it, Cain chose his own course.

Later, God confronted Cain again: "Where is your brother Abel?" (Genesis 4:9).

Cain's response to God is classic. It echoes throughout history to this very day. It lays bare the competitive, self-deceiving soul of a man.

"Am I my brother's keeper?" You can hear the *attitude* in his reply.
"How should I know where Abel is?"
"He's not my responsibility!"
"Frankly, it's none of my business!"
"Go ask someone else!"
"I've got myself to think about."
"Get off my back!"

In Cain's mind, the vivid pictures were playing the whole time: the place where he bent to pick up the stone, his quiet approach, the stunned look on Abel's face, the blood. . . . The truth of what was in his heart had burst into violent life: the first murder. Maybe Cain had been shocked by it himself.

And now he tries to hide the memory-images—the truth about himself—even from God. But it cannot be done.

> The Lord said, "What have you done? Listen! Your brother's blood cries out to me from the ground. Now you are under a curse and driven from the ground, which opened its mouth to receive your brother's blood from your hand. When

you work the ground, it will no longer yield its crops for you. You will be a restless wanderer on the earth" (Genesis 4:10–12).

Cain was not only the first murderer, he was the first man who chose to live brotherless. The first man who thought he could make a go of it on his own. The first man who hated losing the comparison game so much he chose isolation over brotherhood. As a result, Cain found himself under a curse. Soon he would feel other effects of his sin-guilt. The inability to build healthy relationships made him a "restless wanderer," rather than a well-friended man, living at peace with other men before God.

The Answer Is "YES"

Cain's question to God was, "Am I my brother's keeper?" God's answer—throughout the whole of Scripture and to every one of us—is "Yes, you are!" We do have a responsibility to our brothers. And we *need* to avoid isolation by building bridges into the lives of other men. Consider the promises of God that invite us to spiritual brotherhood:

- "How good and how pleasant it is for brethren to dwell together in unity! . . . for there the LORD commanded the blessing; life forevermore" (Psalm 133:1, 3, NKJV).
- "As iron sharpens iron, so one man sharpens another" (Proverbs 27:17).
- "Greater love has no one than this, that he lay down his life for his friends" (John 15:13).
- "By this all men will know that you are my disciples, if you love one another" (John 13:35).
- "Let us consider how we may spur one another on toward love and good deeds. Let us not give up meeting together, as some are in the habit of doing, but let us encourage one another—and all the more as you see the Day [of the Lord's return] approaching" (Hebrews 10:24–25).
- "Love the brotherhood of believers" (1 Peter 2:17).
- "Be devoted to one another in brotherly love. Honor one another above yourselves" (Romans 12:10).
- "Confess your sins to each other and pray for each other so that you may be healed" (James 5:16).
- "For where two or three come together in my name, there am I with them" (Matthew 18:20).

SOUL OPENER

Breakfast of Champions

If you recognize your need for Christ-honoring man-to-man friendships, you may be asking, "How do I enlist? What will it take to find the right brother to befriend?" The following suggestions will help you in the process:

1. *Pray.* Ask God to lead you to the right Christian man or group of men. Invite your wife to pray with you about this need.

2. *Seek the counsel of a trusted pastor or Christian leader.* Sit down and discuss the need for support, encouragement, and godly wisdom with him. Prayerfully consider his counsel, and ask for help in getting a small men's fellowship started, if one does not exist.

3. *If you do not belong to a local Christian church, seek out one that has an active men's ministry.* Then get involved!

4. *Set up a fellowship group with another man.* If you are already aware of another man or two who have the makings of solid brothers in Christ, give it a trial run. Informally meet with them, and get to know each other better. Ask them to commit to a regular place and time every week to encourage one another in everyday challenges and in faith.

5. *Don't give up.* Remember, your first effort at forging deeper friendship may not be the right one. If it doesn't work out, keep trying. The process may not happen right away, but the benefit to your life and family will be well worth it!

Notes

1. "Into-Me-See," by Rod Cooper, *New Man* (Mar-Apr 1995), p. 42.
2. Dee Brestin, *The Friendships of Women* (Wheaton, IL: Victor Books, Scripture Press Publications, Inc., 1988), pp. 14–15.
3. As quoted in *Male-Female Roles*, "Men Need Liberating From Repressed Feelings," by Richard Cohen (St. Paul, MN: Greenhaven Press, 1983), p. 96.

CHAPTER FOURTEEN

Every Man Needs an Armor-Bearer

"What happiness, what confidence, what joy to have a person to whom you dare to speak on terms of equality as to another self. . . . You can entrust all the secrets of your heart to him and before him you can lay out all your plans. . . . No bragging is to be feared and no suspicion need be feared."

—Aelred of Rievaulx

One definition of armor-bearer: *a comrade who accompanies a man into battle, supplies him with needed weapons, and lifts his soul.*

Tom Clancy has captured the souls and minds of millions of male readers, and some women as well. Carving out a new genre, the "techno-thriller," Clancy weaves page-turners that are hard to put down. His lead characters appear as "everyday Joes" who have more integrity in their back pockets than they can find anywhere in their government. Publishers tell us that men don't like to read—and if they choose to read they don't like thick books or long chapters. Clancy takes his audience through hundreds of pages and, in part, his magic comes from allowing us to come alongside another man—a good man surrounded by danger and corruption. Soon we're pulling for him as if our own life were at stake.

In the hills of ancient Palestine, just before David rose to power, we find another man worthy of our admiration and interest. A true hero who wanted only to serve his nation and be a good friend. Like the leads in Clancy's novels, he is heroic and courageous, yet humble and a bit inconspicuous. The difference is that this man actually lived.

His name we do not know—but he was an armor-bearer to Jonathan, the son of King Saul and a renowned warrior. With patient endurance, this man went into battle with Jonathan against the Philistines, a notorious group of bloodthirsty guerrilla warriors who had taken ground that belonged to Israel.

Consider the incredible service of this man:

> Now a detachment of Philistines had gone out to the pass at Micmash. One day Jonathan son of Saul said to the young man bearing his armor . . . "Come, let's go over to the outpost of those uncircumcised fellows. Perhaps the Lord will act in our behalf. Nothing can hinder the Lord from saving, whether by many or by few."
>
> "Do all that you have in mind," his armor-bearer said, "Go ahead; I am with you heart and soul. . . ."
>
> So both of them showed themselves to the Philistine outpost. "Look!" said the Philistines. "The Hebrews are crawling out of the holes they were hiding in." The men . . . shouted to Jonathan and his armor-bearer. "Come up to us and we'll teach you a lesson."
>
> So Jonathan said to his armor-bearer, "Climb up after me; the Lord has given them into the hand of Israel."
>
> Jonathan climbed up . . . with his armor-bearer right behind him. The Philistines fell before Jonathan, and his armor-bearer followed and killed behind him. In that first attack Jonathan and his armor-bearer killed some twenty men in an area of about half an acre. Then panic struck the whole [Philistine] army . . . and the ground shook. It was a panic sent by God (see 1 Samuel 13:23–14:15).

Facing battle odds of ten-to-one, these two men demonstrate a principle every one of us needs to live by: *No man can afford to be without an armor-bearer.*

The Buddy System

One soldier recalls the impact of having an armor-bearer in his life:

> If it hadn't been for Stevie McDonald, I don't know if I would have made it. Trauma tumbled upon trauma. Adversity heaped upon adversity. Obstacle stacked upon obstacle. Test piled upon test. It was way too much for one soldier to handle.
>
> Especially a little soldier.
>
> It wasn't just the tense teachers and emotional moms that got to me. There were lines. Mats. Desks. Rules. Order.

Explanations. And girls—more girls than I'd ever seen in one place.

But somehow, on that first terrifying day of kindergarten, Stevie and I found each other and huddled together like a couple of lost puppies. Together, we survived the stress. We even traded snacks! That may have been the first time I experienced the soul-buttressing impact of what I call "mutual mentoring." But it wasn't the last.

Years later, in 1967, a grizzled old noncom at Fort Benning, Georgia, taught the same principles—in a different way—to a formation of ramrod-straight troops: "Never go into battle alone!"[1]

In ancient Hebrew culture, an armor-bearer was a man who assisted a warrior with his weaponry—which could be quite heavy and burdensome—and he also often fought along with him. As the Bible shows us, an armor-bearer not only carried armor—in a sense, he *carried the soul* of the man to whom he was committed, supporting, encouraging, and cheering him on to victory. Armor-bearers were selected because they were men of great strength and character, able in battle, and deeply loyal in spirit. Jonathan won, in part, because of the soul-support he received from his armor-bearer.

All over America today, men are finding more courage to face the battles of life than they ever dreamed possible. How? By building relationships with fellow armor-bearers—with brothers in Christ who are committed to meeting regularly, influencing one another's lives, praying for each other, and challenging one another to be faithful to God, to family, and to church.

We can learn a lot about helping each other from Jonathan's unnamed armor-bearer.

Lessons for Brothers in Battle

First, armor-bearers help us anticipate attacks. In the face of bloodthirsty Philistines, Jonathan not only drew his weapons from his "wingman," he planned his battle strategy with him, as well. The armorbearer was a confidant with whom Jonathan could discuss and weigh his options before jumping into the fray. This trusted ally provided another set of eyes and instincts to help refine his own thoughts.

We need spiritual brothers to give us other perspectives and add broader experience to our strategies as we face all of life's challenges.

Second, armor-bearers equip us to see with spiritual eyes. Jonathan said to his young armor-bearer, "Come, let's go over to the outpost of those uncircumcised fellows." While most men feared the numbers and weaponry of the Philistine army, in the company of his armor-bearer Jonathan was able to consider something more significant—their spiritual condition, which was in opposition to the Lord.

Armor-bearers are men who—by their own commitment to God—stir us to look beyond our outward circumstances and to consider their spiritual significance.

Third, armor-bearers inspire us to expect the intervention of God in our lives. "Perhaps the Lord will act in our behalf," said Jonathan. The power of *expectant faith* is too often snuffed out by words of doubt and uncertainty. Fear and doubt cause us to say, "I can't . . ." "I've never . . ." "I'm not sure I . . ." and "Why should I. . . ?"

With the support of his armor-bearer and confidant, Jonathan pondered the possibility—make that the *impossibility*—of two men facing the entire Philistine army. But more than that, he was inspired to consider the Lord of heaven and earth, the God with whom all things are possible!

Fourth, armor-bearers know that God's most formidable weapon is two or three men who truly believe. "Nothing can hinder the Lord from saving, whether by many or by few," Jonathan insisted.

I am told that early on in the life of Youth for Christ Ministries, during one of their national conventions, a handful of eager and energetic young men took advantage of some free time. They climbed up onto an overlook area and began to talk, dream, and pray together about how God might use their lives. Each one expressed his desire to touch the world for God's glory and to serve His purposes. These few young men were Billy Graham, Ted Engstrom (former president of World Vision), Jay Kessler (former president of Youth for Christ), and Bill Bright (founder of Campus Crusade for Christ).

These men—warriors and armor-bearers all—have indeed touched the world for God's glory. Millions, touched by a few.

Fifth, armor-bearers find their success in making their brothers successful. "Do all that you have in mind," his armor-bearer said. "Go ahead; I am with you heart and soul."

Vince Lombardi's legendary Green Bay Packers ruled the gridiron in the 1960s. More importantly, they did it *together.* Lombardi characterized their secret as "fond affection." He insisted upon it as an essential ingredient for a team tough enough to make it to the Super Bowl. His words say it best: "You've got to care for one another. You have to love one another. Each player has to be thinking about the next guy. The difference between mediocrity and greatness is the feeling these players have for one another. Most people call it team spirit. When the players are imbued with that special feeling, you know you have yourself a winning team."

One soldier discovered the same principles in a different area:

> The war in Vietnam was building to its peak, and one stop for young army officers was the J.S. Army Ranger School at Fort Benning. The venerable, steely-eyed veteran told us the next nine weeks would test our mettle as it had never been tested.
>
> The sergeant said many would not make the grade—it was just too tough. (Turned out he was right. Of 287 in the formation that day, only 110 finished the nine weeks.)
>
> I can still hear that raspy voice cutting through the morning humidity like a serrated blade. "We are here to save your lives," he preached. "We're going to see to it that you overcome all your natural fears—especiallly of height and water. We're going to show you just how much incredible stress the human mind and body can endure. And when we're finished with you, you will be the U.S. Army's best. You will not only survive in combat, you will accomplish your mission!"
>
> Then, before he dismissed the formation, the hardened Ranger Sergeant announced our first assignment. We'd steeled ourselves for something really tough—running ten miles in full battle gear or rappelling down a sheer cliff. So the noncom's first order caught us off guard.
>
> He told us to find a buddy. Some of us would have preferred the cliff.
>
> "This is step one," he growled. "You need to find yourself a Ranger buddy. You will stick together. You will never leave each other. You will encourage each other and, as necessary, you will carry each other."
>
> It was the Army's way of saying, *Difficult assignments require a friend. Together is better. You need someone to help you accomplish the tough course ahead.*[2]

Armor-bearers are not just acquainted with each other—they are committed to each other "heart and soul."

Sixth, armor-bearers challenge us to take the steps we would otherwise never take on our own. So Jonathan said to his armor-bearer, "Climb up after me; the LORD has given them into the hand of Israel." Every man needs a friend who will encourage and challenge him to grow up as a man and as a Christian.

One way an armor-bearer challenges his brother-in-Christ is by asking him great questions. Dream-revealing questions. Laziness-exposing questions. Creative-solution questions.

An armor-bearer does not impose answers, he helps steer you to answers.

Seventh, armor-bearers never have to fight alone. "Jonathan climbed up . . . with his armor-bearer right behind him." The Philistines fell before Jonathan, and his armor-bearer followed and killed behind him.

In his infinite wisdom, God has designed us in such a way that we do not function at a premium alone. Not only has he formed men to need friendships, but he chooses to bless such friendships.

God is calling men to become armor-bearers for one another in the real adventure of life.

SOUL OPENERS

Twenty-five Questions Men Need to Be Asked

1. What dynamics in your life work most against your becoming a more faithful man of God? What are you up against?

2. How do you guard yourself morally? What steps do you regularly take to keep your thought life and lifestyle in check and strong spiritually?

3. To whom are you accountable as a man? Whom have you given permission to ask you the hard questions?

4. If someone were to ask your kids, "How do you know that your dad loves you?" what would they say?

5. If your family was arrested for being Christian, would there be enough "evidence" to convict you? What about your family reveals that it is truly "Christian"?

6. What does your wife most need from you as a husband?

7. What convictions/values are you passing on to your kids? Are they catching them? How can you tell?

8. What place does prayer have in your marriage?

9. Do you effectively move from a work-orientation to a family-orientation on your way home?

10. When you inappropriately "lose your cool" or unload on your kids, do you apologize to them? Why/Why not? What usually results?

11. If someone asked your wife, "How do you know that your husband loves you?" what would she say?

12. Have you ever caught yourself living out of your anger? What does it look like? How does it show itself? What does it produce in your family? Your co-workers?

13. What are currently the greatest sources of ongoing frustration in your life? What are you doing to cope?

14. When did God become more than just a name to you?

15. What did your parents do to help "aim" your life as a child? (See Psalm 127:3–5). What are you doing to help aim your children?

16. What blessing do you most tend to take for granted in your life?

17. What kind of old man do you want to be one day?

18. What is the most meaningful time you have ever spent with your son/daughter? What made it so special?

19. How do you pray for your kids? What kinds of things do you ask God for as it relates to their lives?

20. Whom do you admire the most in life? Whom is it that you would most want to be like? What is it about this person that intrigues you most?

21. As a provider, what does a family need the most from the man of the house?

22. What do you do for fun? How often do you work this into your schedule?

23. What is the most thoughtful thing you did for your wife this week?

24. What is the most thoughtful thing you did for your kids this week?

25. What makes a man a man of God? What does it involve?

Notes

1. "Some One to Lean On" by Stu Weber in *Focus on the Family* magazine (June 1996), p. 2.
2. Ibid., pp.2 3.

Conclusion
Souled Out!

The path God has us on as men is best lived as we live more deeply connected to Him—and less selfishly. Jesus said, "If anyone would come after me, he must deny himself and take up his cross and follow me" (Mark 8:34). In a world that takes, Jesus counseled us to give. When we do, we have more room to receive.

We look at Jesus and see a man stepping away from His own interests. Washing feet. Feeding the hungry. Teaching the unlearned. Defending the oppressed. Praying. Fasting. Dealing with people who are hard to deal with. All the while expanding His soul to reach even more. Not as interested in being served as in serving (Mark 10:45).

Here are a few ways a man who wants to serve Christ and others can stretch his soul (and I'm sure there are thousands of others):

- *Reflect more.* If we would stop and *prayerfully consider* more often, I am certain we would be much more in step with God. Quietness before God is all about breaking free of that automatic tendency we have of doing things our way.
- *Take some risks.* Jesus had low tolerance for men who simply played it safe. Smug. Self-determined. The question to consider is: When was the last time you did something for the first time for Jesus' sake? Break out of the bubble of your own self-focused world. There are other worlds to explore.
- *Give generously.* In a world that teaches us to count our own income and our own expenses, spend a day counting the needs of people around you. Devote some of your resources to those needs and watch how God uses it to open and free your heart.
- *Lavish love.* I know things may be tight financially. And yes, there are other expenses to tend to. But, when is the last time you cut loose and did something fun and crazy with your spouse? A romantic get-

away. A night on the town. An unexpected gift for no special occasion. Oswald Chambers said, "If human love does not carry a man beyond himself, it is not love. If love is always discreet, always wise, always sensible and calculating, never carried beyond itself, it is not love at all. It may be affection, it may be warmth of feeling, but it has not the true nature of love in it." Love was meant to be lavished, not trickled.

- *Watch your kids.* Really watch them! Take some time—put the ledgers and papers and remotes and computer mouses down. Watch your toddler live his life for a few minutes. Look at your grade-schooler playing a game. Look at your teen while she is doing her homework. Look long enough to remember—to remember just how incredibly important, precious, and valuable they are to you. And don't just look—make yourself available to help, and do, and play, and listen.

- *Practice His presence.* Take some time today to ask God to make himself known to you more fully. Tell Him that as a son, you want to get to know Him better. Then talk with Him. Thank Him for everything you can think of that He has done for you and given you. Then prayerfully read His Word, the Bible. Stop and think, I mean really think: *How can I experience and obey these insights?*

- *Get involved in helping someone in need.* They are all around you. Be a big brother to the son of a single parent. Help out at the homeless meal event in your community. Volunteer to assist your neighbor on the new deck he's building, or on that paint job. Don't just snow-blow your own driveway—do the old man's down the street, too.

- *Lighten your load; live simply.* Is there something you own that is causing you more headache than it's worth? Do you really need it? Sell it or give it away. Use the time you spent on that project for something that carries more eternal value. Or simply give yourself a break. Rest from it.

- *Go after a dream.* Oswald Chambers said it best: "If you ever had a vision from God and you try to live on a level lower than that, God will never allow it." Ask God for permission. Then start the pursuit. Finish that project. Start that ministry. Phone a friend. Make that contact. Apply for that job. Don't be content to watch an adventure video. Live one. Be bold!

- *Strike up a new friendship.* This may be the most challenging step a man will ever take. I am convinced, however, that it can be the most rewarding. If you sense the need for a brother-friendship, don't just seek for one—*be* one. Our planet is covered with more brotherless men than fatherless. Take a step. Ask a question. Get interested. Care. You and I both need an armor-bearer.

———

In the final analysis, growing in God is all about stretching our souls. Working out the gifts that God has invested in us.

Today, and every day, determine to live your life deeply, richly—*from the soul*.

Discussion Questions

Chapter One—Living Life From the Soul

1. What are some of the ways soldiers, prizefighters, and NFL football players get themselves "psyched-up" before facing their opponents? What are their techniques?
2. Does your soul work more like a "thermostat" or a "thermometer"? Does your emotional "temperature" remain quite constant, or do your surroundings cause it to fluctuate?
3. In what ways as a man do you tend to go to extremes? What do you think causes this?
4. In the past twenty-four hours, what have you been "living out of"? What has motivated most of your activity? How can you tell?
5. What intrigues you the most about the Bible character Stephen? What would it take for you to be more like him?
6. Which weaknesses in the character of Saul of Tarsus do you most identify with as a man? Where do you think they come from? What will it take to shake these?
7. God confronted Saul on the road to Damascus. Have you ever faced a season in your life in which you felt you were being confronted by God? How could you tell? What was it like? Ultimately, how did it affect your life?

Chapter Two—Soul at War

1. What does a "successful" man look like, according to our culture? Describe him.
2. Paul (formerly Saul of Tarsus) as a Christian expressed the fact that he still struggled greatly as a man. What aspects of his account of that struggle in Romans 7:14–24 remind you the most of yourself? How?

3. Soul is a word with which our culture seems to be endeavoring to get reacquainted. In your own words, what is a soul? What does it consist of and what is its function and purpose?
4. In what ways are men in our world today doing what Jesus warned against: gaining "the world" and losing their "own souls"?
5. What does sin do to a man's soul? Can you think of an example in which you have observed or experienced this tragic process?
6. When God confronted the murderer Cain before his crime, He said, "Sin is crouching at your door, it desires to have you, but you must master it (Genesis 4:7).

- What was the sin "crouching" at the door of Cain's soul?
- In what ways did the voice of God sound like a coach in this instance?
- What was God commanding when He said, "You must master it"?

7. What do faith, hope, and love do for a man's soul? What will it take to see them strengthened in your life?

Chapter Three—Snapshots of the Soul Set Free

1. Who was the most courageous man in American history? Why do you think he was?
2. In your opinion, how accurate is the quote by Richard Foster that appears at the beginning of this chapter? How many truly "deep" people do you know? How can you tell they are deep? What makes them that way?
3. With regard to his purpose for living, who is the most passionate man you know? What do you admire most about him?
4. Why do you think it is hard for a man to say, "I need help!"?
5. If emotions are what bring color to our lives, would you describe yours as "black and white," "Technicolor," or "somewhere in between"?
6. What does our culture tell men to do with their emotions? What does the example of Christ tell us to do with them?
7. Have you ever met a truly meek man? What set him apart from other men you have known?
8. If money were no issue, what would your ultimate adventure vacation look like? Where would you go and what would you do?
9. For whom do you have the most compassion today? For whom do you have the least? What does this tell you about yourself?
10. Would you describe the conscience you have today as strong, weak, or seared? What brings you to this conclusion?
11. What influences in your life have most shaped your conscience?

What are you doing to strengthen the consciences of your children?

12. In what way is the Christian life like the work of a bridge builder? What "bridges" are the strongest in your life? Which "bridges" around you need repair?

13. How do you deal with the "down times" in your life? Can you imagine being able to rejoice in the midst of one?

14. One of Jesus' favorite expressions to His followers was "Be of good cheer." What brings you the greatest joy most often in life?

Chapter Four—Opening a Man's Soul

1. What is the meanest thing you ever did as a kid? What inspired you?

2. Jesus said, "Nothing outside a man can make him 'unclean'. . . . Rather, it is what comes out of a man that makes him 'unclean' " (Mark 7:14–15). What kinds of things do you see "coming out" of the men around you most often at work? at church? at ball games?

3. In what way is "a man who controls his temper (better) than one who takes a city"? (Proverbs 16:32).

4. Describe the two rivers found in Galatians 5:19–23. Which one is flowing out of your life? How do you know this?

5. What "broken" experience in your life has God used the most to open your soul? Explain.

6. Have you ever thought of God as the "engineer of your circumstances"? How does that concept strike you?

7. Do you have a real soul-brother in your life? In what ways does he help you in your spiritual journey?

Chapter Five—A Twig in the Cement

1. In the story *Pinnochio*, Jiminy Cricket is the young boy's conscience. Who has come the closest to being yours?

2. Define the word "integrity." What does it mean?

3. Today, are most men "integers" or "fractions" spiritually? What gives them away?

4. In what ways does "image" get in the way of integrity?

5. What impresses you about Daniel and the life he lived? Are there any public leaders today who remind you of him?

6. What have been the biggest tests of integrity you have faced to date? How did you fare?

7. Which of the three blessings for the man of integrity intrigues you the most? Why?

8. Are you more oriented toward grace or truth? Explain.

Chapter Six—The Fire in Your Soul

1. Have you ever had an extreme encounter with an angry man, such as the one Bob Crosby cited? If so, how did it make you feel? What did you do about it?
2. What was Moses' "Achilles heel"? In what way did it get the best of him?
3. Have you ever tried to do God's will *your* way? How does God look upon such an approach? (Isaiah 55:8–9).
4. What kinds of situations tend to trigger anger in your life most often? How do they generally develop?
5. What do you usually do with your anger?
6. Have you ever considered that anger and anxiety are "prayer triggers"? What do you think of this concept?

Chapter Seven—The Ultimate Power Tool

1. In your estimation, who is the most powerful man in the world? Why do you think so?
2. In what ways is our culture obsessed with power? What are the telltale signs?
3. How has power or control been an issue for you in
   - your marriage?
   - your career?
   - your role as a parent?
4. Would you consider the kind of love that Jesus taught to be a powerful tool? How?
5. Tony Campolo says, "A craving for power interferes with love and destroys personal relationships." Have you experienced this? In what ways?
6. What is the "ultimate power tool"? Is it a part of your life's toolbox?
7. Read through the "Bosses vs. Leaders" list again. Is this list accurate in your experience?

Chapter Eight—As for Me and My House

1. How do contemporary television shows portray father figures? Cite some of the current shows and describe the male leads and their profiles. What does this say about our culture's opinion of men?
2. What impact did Adam's fall have on the psyche ("soul") of man? How does it affect you today as a man and the way you live your life?
3. Would you describe your dad as being "engaged" or disengaged"

as a father during your childhood? What is the basis for your assessment?
4. Who taught you how to be a husband? how to be a dad? Who was or is your mentor? Where do you go when you need wisdom?
5. What characteristics of Joshua do you most admire? Why?
6. Do you have a vision for your family? for your marriage? for your kids? What are they?
7. Are you able to "fully engage" your wife and kids when you get home from work? If so, how do you do it?

Chapter Nine—Naked . . . and Unashamed
1. Before sin entered the Garden, how could Adam and Eve possibly have been naked and "unashamed"? To what do you attribute this?
2. Why do women tend to be more vulnerable and open with their lives than men?
3. Which requires more courage: concealing a fear or confessing it? Why is this true?
4. Who do you allow to enter the "holy of holies" of your own heart and soul?
5. Are you comfortable talking about your fears? your dreams? your aspirations? your faith? your failures? Why or why not?
6. How would you define intimacy? Is it something you need? Explain.

Chapter Ten—Strengthening Your Soul Mate
1. Have you ever received a message from your wife similar to the one Bob Crosby received from his? How did you respond?
2. If your wife were to write you an honest letter today about your marriage, what do you think she would say?
3. In what ways did the Fall of man make marriage even more complicated? How did it put men and women at odds with each other?
4. Who is most responsible for cultivating a marriage and building it, the husband or the wife? Why is this true?
5. What does your wife need most from you as a husband? What are you doing about that today?
6. What does it mean to wash your wife with the Word of God? Have you ever done this? How did you do it? What effect did it have on her? (Ephesians 5:25–30).

Chapter Eleven—Father, Guide, and Helper
1. In what ways has becoming a dad stretched you as a man? as a Christian?

2. In what ways does your household function like a church?
3. Which statements and observations from the "Out of the Mouths of Ten-Year-Olds" section most caught your attention? Do you agree with the assessment? Why?
4. What role does encouragement play in your home? What are you doing as a dad to plant it in the atmosphere regularly? What is the most encouraging thing you have said to your son or daughter this week?
5. Do you expect too much from your kids or not enough? Explain.
6. In what ways do your expectations impact your children and their souls?
7. What does it take for a man to truly take the lead in his home? What are the essentials?
8. How can a man keep his son's or daughter's soul "open"? What does it take?

Chapter Twelve—Leading Your Household to God
1. When do you feel the most "together" as a family? When are you the closest to one another?
2. What is the most meaningful time of spiritual devotion you have ever shared with your family? What made it so great?
3. Is there any ingredient more essential to your home and family life than having meaningful times of spiritual instruction and prayer? What kinds of things usually get in the way of you doing so?
4. Are you comfortable with leading family devotions? Why or why not?
5. What resources do you have available to assist you in leading family devotions?
6. Should the husband always lead the devotional times with his family? Why or why not?
7. How can you have meaningful devotions when the kids are bouncing off the walls?

Chapter Thirteen—"Am I My Brother's Keeper?"
1. How do you feel when you get on an elevator—relaxed or uncomfortable? Why is this?
2. Do you have any men whom you would truly consider "close friends"? What characterizes these relationships?
3. What keeps men from building strong friendships?
4. In what ways does competitiveness among men work against meaningful friendships?

5. Are you your brother's keeper? What is the answer to that eternal question?
6. What is it like for a man to live life without a brother? How does it affect the quality of his life? his marriage? his fathering? his soul?

Chapter Fourteen—Every Man Needs an Armor-Bearer

1. What is your favorite Tom Clancy novel or movie? What did you like the most about it?
2. In a fighter jet squadron, how important is the camaraderie between a lead man and a wingman? What does it take for them to perform well when they actually engage the enemy?
3. In a sport, job, or assignment, have you ever had another man who served as your "wingman"? or whom you served as a "wingman"? In what way?
4. In what ways are you as a man "in battle" or "at war" every day?
5. Do you have an "armor-bearer" friendship? If so, describe it.
6. In what ways would a true armor-bearer enhance your life today?
7. What steps will you take to build a true "armor-bearer" friendship?